Margaret Mitchell's

Gone With the Wind

Text by
Gail Rae Rosensfit
(M.A., Hunter College)
Department of English
McKee Vocational Technical High School
Staten Island, New York

Illustrations by
Karen Pica

Research & Education Association

MAXnotes™ for
GONE WITH THE WIND

Printed in the United States of America

Library of Congress Catalog Card Number 94-65962

International Standard Book Number 0-87891-955-4

MAXnotes™ is a trademark of
Research & Education Association, Piscataway, New Jersey 08854

What MAXnotes™ Will Do for You

This book is intended to help you absorb the essential contents and features of Margaret Mitchell's *Gone With the Wind* and to help you gain a thorough understanding of the work. The book has been designed to do this more quickly and effectively than any other study guide.

For best results, this **MAXnotes** book should be used as a companion to the actual work, not instead of it. The interaction between the two will greatly benefit you.

To help you in your studies, this book presents the most up-to-date interpretations of every section of the actual work, followed by questions and fully explained answers that will enable you to analyze the material critically. The questions also will help you to test your understanding of the work and will prepare you for discussions and exams.

Meaningful illustrations are included to further enhance your understanding and enjoyment of the literary work. The illustrations are designed to place you into the mood and spirit of the work's settings.

The **MAXnotes** also include summaries, character lists, explanations of plot, and chapter-by-chapter analyses. A biography of the author and discussion of the work's historical context will help you put this literary piece into the proper perspective of what is taking place.

The use of this study guide will save you the hours of preparation time that would ordinarily be required to arrive at a complete grasp of this work of literature. You will be well-prepared for classroom discussions, homework, and exams. The guidelines that are included for writing papers and reports on various topics will prepare you for any added work which may be assigned.

The **MAXnotes** will take your grades "to the max."

Dr. Max Fogiel
Program Director

Contents

Section One: *Introduction* 1

   The Life and Work of Margaret Mitchell 1

   Historical Background 2

   Master List of Characters 3

   Summary of the Novel 5

   Estimated Reading Time 6

Each chapter includes List of Characters, Summary, Analysis, Study Questions and Answers, and Suggested Essay Topics.

Section Two: *Gone with the Wind, Part I* 7

   Chapter 1 7

   Chapter 2 10

   Chapters 3-5 12

   Chapters 6-7 15

Section Three: *Gone with the Wind, Part II* 21

   Chapters 8-10 21

   Chapters 11-13 26

   Chapters 14-16 31

Section Four: *Gone with the Wind, Part III* 37

    Chapters 17-18 37

    Chapters 19-22 42

    Chapters 23-25 45

    Chapters 26-28 51

    Chapters 29-30 55

Section Five: *Gone with the Wind, Part IV* 61

    Chapters 31-32 61

    Chapters 33-34 65

    Chapters 35-36 70

    Chapters 37-38 75

    Chapters 39-42 80

    Chapters 43-45 87

    Chapters 46-47 94

Section Six: *Gone with the Wind, Part V* 99

    Chapters 48-50 99

    Chapters 51-53 105

    Chapters 54-56 111

    Chapters 57-59 116

    Chapters 60-63 121

Section Seven: *Sample Analytical Paper Topics* 126

Section Eight: *Bibliography* 130

Introduction

The Life and Work of Margaret Mitchell

Margaret Mitchell wrote only one book, *Gone with the Wind*, and won a Pulitzer Prize for fiction in 1937, as well as the National Book Award. Written in 1936, *Gone with the Wind* set a sales record of 50,000 copies in one day and 1.5 million copies in its first year of publication, making it one of the most successful bestsellers ever written. It has been translated into at least 30 languages, including Braille (becoming the longest novel ever translated into this language). In 1939, the book was used as the basis of what is probably the most popular film ever made.

Born in Atlanta, Georgia, which she uses for the setting of her story, on November 8, 1900, Ms. Mitchell wrote this novel over a period of 10 years, after her marriage to John March in 1925. During this time, she wove material from the stories of the Civil War she had heard at home (as the daughter of the president of the Atlanta Historical Society) into this historical novel of over 1,000 pages, written from the Southern point of view; local history had been a pervasive part of her childhood. The story, itself, begins just before the Civil War in 1861 and ends during the Reconstruction period. Her two main characters—Scarlett O'Hara and Rhett Butler—are among the best-known in American literature.

Although she attended Smith College during 1918-1919, when her mother died she returned home to keep house for her father and brother. On August 16, 1949, a car struck Ms. Mitchell, ending her life. In 1976, Margaret Mitchell's Gone *with the Wind Letters: 1936-1949*was published. A continuation of the novel, *Scarlett: The Sequel to Margaret Mitchell's Gone with the Wind*, written by Alexandra Ripley, was published in 1991.

Historical Background

In April 1861, the Civil War began when the Confederacy bombarded Fort Sumter in South Carolina. President Lincoln declared war, called for 75,000 volunteers (for 90-day enlistments), and blockaded Southern ports. Virginia, Arkansas, North Carolina, and Tennessee soon joined the Confederacy, while the border states of Maryland, Missouri, and Kentucky became a major concern for both presidents.

In July of 1862, Lincoln announced the Emancipation Proclamation, dashing any hopes the Confederacy had of military aid from Great Britain or France, who could not support the endorsement of human bondage by the South (since they now saw the Civil War as a struggle to end slavery). Up to this point, the war had been seen as a means to save the Union. A military policy used by the North was to strip Southern plantations of their labor supply as an economic sanction.

Another policy was the use of blockades which kept the cotton in, the foreign military supplies out, and hindered the South by cutting into the supply lines. The Confederacy was doing poorly before the war: currency was almost worthless since it had never been declared legal tender and shortages were rampant.

When the war ended in 1865, the South was ravished: farms, homes, and places of business in ruins; people missing; the land and people exhausted; slavery demolished; and the great plantations gone.

Lincoln had high hopes for the reconstruction of the South, beginning with his 1/10 Plan, according to which when one-tenth of the qualified Southern voters for the year 1860 took an oath of loyalty to the Constitution, they would be permitted to set up state governments and ask for recognition by the federal government. When this was done, he intended to use his presidential power of pardon to restore full rights.

After Lincoln's assassination, President Andrew Johnson continued this policy. By 1871, all the states were part of the federal government again.

In March of 1867, Congress legislated dividing the South into five military districts, each commanded by a general. With Grant's presidency, Northern carpetbaggers appeared throughout the South, occupying key offices and controlling the political apparatus. They were aided by Southern Scalawags, there for their own personal gain. Buying and selling the votes of the newly enfranchised became common.

When Rutherford B. Hayes was elected president in 1876, the last army units from the South were recalled, causing the entire false economy to collapse and reconstruction (which failed politically, socially, and economically) to end.

Master List of Characters

(Katie) Scarlett O'Hara—the protagonist of the novel; born to the luxury of pre-Civil War plantation life in Georgia; eldest daughter of Gerald and Ellen O'Hara; wife of Charles Hamilton, Frank Kennedy, and Rhett Butler; mother of Wade Hampton Hamilton, Ella Lorna Kennedy, and Eugenie Victoria Butler.

Ellen Robillard O'Hara—Scarlett's mother; a respected woman who raises her daughters to be Southern ladies.

Gerald O'Hara—Scarlett's father; an Irish immigrant and self-made man.

(Susan Elinor) Suellen O'Hara—Scarlett's younger sister; engaged to Frank Kennedy for many years before Scarlett marries him; marries Will Benteen.

(Caroline Irene) Carreen O'Hara—the youngest of the three O'Hara sisters; becomes a nun after the death of her beloved, Brent Tarleton, in the Civil War.

Mammy—body slave of Ellen O'Hara's mother; raises Ellen, Ellen's three daughters, and Scarlett's children.

Pork—Gerald O'Hara's body slave; survives both Gerald and Ellen; continues to help keep the family plantation, Tara, from falling into Union hands during the Civil War years.

Dilcey—Pork's wife; bought by Gerald from John Wilkes' neighboring plantation, Twelve Oaks, to honor Pork's request that the newlyweds may live together.

Prissy—Dilcey's daughter; also purchased by Gerald as a surprise for Pork when he buys Dilcey.

Ashley Wilkes—a neighbor Scarlett convinces herself she loves although he is to marry his cousin from Atlanta, Melanie Hamilton.

(Melanie) Melly Hamilton Wilkes—Ashley's wife; becomes Scarlett's greatest defender and sister-in-law when Scarlett marries Melanie's brother, Charles.

(Beauregard) Beau Wilkes—Ashley and Melanie's only child; born during the burning of Atlanta by the Union Army.

Honey Wilkes—one of Ashley's sisters.

India Wilkes—another of Ashley's sisters; becomes one of Scarlett's many enemies in Atlanta.

Charles Hamilton—Scarlett's first husband; tricked into marrying her as revenge when she realizes Ashley really is going to marry Melanie, Charles' sister.

Wade Hampton Hamilton—Scarlett and Charles' son; born after Charles' death of pneumonia following measles while serving in the Confederate Army.

(Sarah Jane) Pittypat Hamilton—Charles and Melanie's spinster aunt; Scarlett lives with her in Atlanta while mourning Charles' death; Ashley, India, and Honey Wilkes' cousin.

Henry Hamilton—Charles and Melanie's uncle; constantly at odds with his sister, Pittypat; the family lawyer.

Uncle Peter—Pittypat's faithful slave.

Frank Kennedy—Scarlett's second husband; owns a store in Atlanta; was engaged to Scarlett's sister, Suellen, for many years before Scarlett tricked him into marriage.

Ella Lorena Kennedy—Frank and Scarlett's daughter.

Rhett Butler—Scarlett's third husband; years before their marriage, befriends and falls in love with Scarlett due to his admiration for her hard business dealings and calculating mind; shunned by society for his scandalous behavior.

(Eugenie Victoria) Bonnie Blue Butler—Rhett and Scarlett's daughter; deeply loved and indulged by Rhett; Scarlett's favorite child.

Mrs. Elsing, Mrs. Merriwether, and Mrs. Whiting—the leaders of Atlanta's society.

Will Benteen—Confederate soldier left at Tara to convalesce from pneumonia; stays to work Tara into a functioning farm; eventually marries Suellen.

Archie—murderer freed from prison for agreeing to fight in the Confederate Army; Melanie employs him as a bodyguard for Scarlett in Atlanta.

Summary of the Novel

Gone with the Wind begins at Tara, the O'Hara family cotton plantation in Georgia, just prior to the Civil War. Hearing the news of Ashley's engagement to Melanie, Scarlett O'Hara tricks Charles Hamilton into marrying her. After Charles' death in the Confederate Army, Melanie (who returns to Atlanta after their marriage and Ashley's enlistment) and Pittypat convince Scarlett to bring her baby for an extended stay. There, she becomes trapped by the war.

On the night of Atlanta's burning by the Union Army, with Melanie having just given birth, Scarlett realizes it is too dangerous to stay. She convinces Rhett Butler to steal a horse and wagon so they may return to Tara. They arrive, without Rhett, to find Ellen dead, Suellen and Carreen ill, Gerald out of his mind, no supplies or horses, very few slaves, and many of the neighboring plantations burned to the ground.

On a return trip to Atlanta to raise the higher taxes newly demanded on Tara by the victors, Scarlett discovers Rhett is in jail. She sees him there and offers herself as collateral for the tax money. Although previously interested, his admiration for her now will not allow this, nor can he reach his money because of the political situation.

Scarlett then lies to Frank Kennedy so that he will marry her.

He has money and a store which promises more if Scarlett's heartless and aggressive business methods are used. Having already been cast from society for her "unwidowlike" behavior, she has no reason not to pursue business. Marrying Frank means another separation from Tara since she will live at Pittypat's house.

Having promised herself she would never be hungry again, Scarlett finds another way of making money by buying and managing two saw mills. Afterwards, she borrows money from Rhett. Frank is not happy, but indulges her, thinking another baby will end such behavior. Ella is born but Scarlett does not convert to contentment with home and family.

In Atlanta, Scarlett continues to do business, despite the dangers of Shantytown, an area through which she must travel inhabited by prostitutes, freed slaves, and lawbreakers. Archie refuses to continue as Scarlett's bodyguard since she exploits ex-convicts who work in the mills. She is then accosted as she passes through Shantytown. Both Ashley and Frank are members of the Ku Klux Klan and feel they must protect her honor. In the fight, Frank is killed and Ashley wounded. Only Rhett's warning and quick thinking save the rest.

Widowed for the second time with two small children, Scarlett marries Rhett and befriends Scalawags and Carpetbaggers. She builds an imitation of southern society around her with Rhett's money and these newly acquired friends. Upon Melanie's death, Scarlett realizes she does not love Ashley but rather Rhett, only to learn that since the death of their daughter, Bonnie (for which Rhett blames himself), he has ceased to love her.

Estimated Reading Time

This is a lengthy book which takes some time to read. We would suggest finding your own pace and reading the book over a period of perhaps 40 hours. Break this into manageable reading periods, five or so chapters at a sitting, to allow yourself to complete the book without reading too much at a time.

Gone with the Wind, Part I

Chapter 1

New Characters:

Scarlet O'Hara: *the protagonist of the novel*

Mammy: *Scarlett's mother's body slave*

Summary

Scarlett O'Hara is discussing with the twins Stuart and Brent Tarleton, her neighbors with whom she flirts despite not being interested in marrying either, their expulsion from the fourth college in two years. They insist it does not matter because the Civil War will soon start. They also tell Scarlett that Ashley plans to announce his engagement to Melanie at a ball the next night. Upon hearing this, Scarlett neglects to invite them to dinner, earning her a lecture on hospitality from Mammy, her mother's body (or personal) slave. The boys leave accompanied by their own body slave, Jeems, but are afraid to face their mother. They go instead to see Abel Wynder, who is in charge of the cavalry troop that has been organized to prepare to fight for the Confederacy.

Analysis

This chapter introduces the plantation lifestyle of pre-Civil War Georgia. Scarlett has been raised by her maternal grandmother's body slave, Mammy, who instructs her in the art of womanhood and sees to her every need. While Scarlett is courted by all the acceptable young men, she secretly chooses Ashley and is stunned that he is to marry the sickly Melanie.

Study Questions

1. At the time the story begins, how old is Scarlett?
2. Why could Stuart and Brent Tarleton not go home yet?
3. How do the twins know of Ashley's engagement?
4. Why does Jeems accompany the twins?
5. Why is Ashley considered "different" from other young men?
6. Why are the officers of The Troop elected by the members?
7. Why is there no need to teach the members of The Troop to shoot?
8. Why doesn't Jeems want to be sent home by himself?
9. Why are the Tarleton twins considered to be desirable husbands?
10. Why doesn't Scarlett want to hear any more talk of the war?

Answers

1. Sixteen is considered the age for being "the belle of the ball," the time to flirt with the young men of your own class in order to attain a proper husband. Scarlett is in all her glory now, enjoying the flirting, the clothes, the intrigues, the parties, and the attention.

2. After being expelled from their fourth college in two years, the Tarleton twins know their mother will not only deny them the Grand Tour of Europe but will be considerably angry since their brothers, Tom and Boyd, left school with them feeling it would not be honorable to stay in a college which expelled their brothers.

3. Pittypat is Charles and Melanie's aunt as well as Ashley's cousin. While at the train station in Atlanta, after being ex-

pelled from the University of Georgia, the twins encounter her and she tells them of the engagement.

4. Body slaves are given to children to be their playmates. As they mature, the body slave accompanies them, waits patiently and silently while they visit, holds their horses, and are in all ways responsible for their masters and mistresses.

5. In pre-Civil War Georgia where plantations are dependent upon slave labor, young gentlemen are expected to enjoy horses, liquor, young ladies, and guns. While Ashley does enjoy each of these somewhat, he much prefers poetry, paintings, and travel.

6. Originally, The Troop was a gentlemen's outfit but did not raise enough men. Soon small farmers, hunters, swamp trappers, and even Crackers, were admitted. They elect officers placing much value on the possession of a cool head and both good marksmanship and equestrian skills.

7. Since Southerners usually hunt, they already know how to shoot. Each household has its own assortment of guns, ranging from the horse pistols of The War of 1812 to the new English rifles.

8. Body slaves are responsible for their owners. Therefore, Jeems feels he will be blamed for allowing the twins to be expelled again and for not bringing them home the night of their visit to Scarlett.

9. "Raising good cotton, riding well, shooting straight, dancing lightly, squiring the ladies with elegance, and carrying one's liquor like a gentleman were the things that mattered," according to the custom of the area at that time. Since the twins could do all of these exceedingly well and prefer doing them, they are desirable as husbands.

10. Scarlett's world consists of barbecues, balls, clothes, elegant dinners, and horseback riding. All of these are considered the realm of a plantation belle; Scarlett prefers to concentrate her energies in these areas.

Chapter 2

New Characters:

Ellen O'Hara: *Scarlett's mother*

Gerald O'Hara: *Scarlett's father*

Summary

After the Tarleton twins leave, Mammy chastises Scarlett for not inviting them to supper and being out in the night air without her shawl. Scarlett realizes it is time for her father to come home and goes to the cedars at the end of the drive to meet him privately. As she waits, she contemplates wanting Ashley and his plans to marry Melanie. Her father arrives drunk and jumps the fence even though he broke his knee doing so the previous year. In return for Scarlett not telling Ellen that Gerald has broken his promise not to jump, he verifies that Ashley's father has told him of the engagement. We learn that Gerald was at Twelve Oaks to buy Dilcey and Prissy so that they could live at Tara with Pork. Through their conversation we discover Scarlett does not share her father's love of the land. As the chapter closes, Ellen is leaving, accompanied by Mammy, to attend to a poor white neighbor, Emmie Slattery, whose baby is dying.

Analysis

Scarlett thinks she has loved Ashley since she first saw him and cannot understand why he does not declare his love, since it is obvious to her that he loves her, too. Gerald is concerned, not only because Scarlett will not accept that Ashley is marrying Melanie, but also because he feels Ashley is not a good match for Scarlett. According to Gerald, Ashley cannot make her happy due to his love for books, poetry and painting which she doesn't share. In addition, he wants to see his daughter marry someone who will add more acreage to Tara and improve the plantation since he intends to bequeath it to her when he dies. Scarlett has no interest in this matter and is aghast at her father's choices for her husband since each of these is not Ashley. Scarlett, in her immaturity, feels she can change Ashley and still wants only him.

Study Questions

1. Why does Scarlett try so hard to please Mammy?

2. Why does Scarlett depend on Gerald to tell the truth about Ashley's engagement?

3. What is Scarlett's opinion of Ashley's interest in writing poetry, reading books, and listening to music?

4. How does Gerald treat Scarlett?

5. Why does Gerald feel Scarlett will never be happy with Ashley?

6. Upon what does Gerald place the highest value?

7. Why does Ellen leave?

8. What are Scarlett's feelings toward her mother?

9. Upon what does Scarlett feel her parents' marriage is based?

10. How do we know Gerald is kindhearted?

Answers

1. Mammy was Ellen's mother's body slave, raised Ellen, and then the O'Hara girls. She feels she should know everything that transpires in these children's lives and, if she does not, will go directly to Ellen who will demand explanations from the girls.

2. Gerald has just spent the afternoon with Ashley's father, John Wilkes.

3. Plantation young men are expected to hunt, gamble, dance, indulge in politics, learn about the plantation, and possibly attend college. Scarlett, herself, has no interest in even talking about reading, much less doing it.

4. Gerald decides to will Tara to Scarlett upon his death. With this in mind, he treats her as a first born son.

5. Gerald knows Scarlett finds Ashley's interest in books, poetry, and music boring and that she will never understand it nor can she change Ashley as she insists she will.

6. As a penniless Irish immigrant, Gerald worked himself into a position to buy Tara and build it into the flourishing plantation it now is. He also contends that land is the only thing that lasts.

7. A poor, white neighbor, Emmie Slattery, has a baby who is dying and needs to be baptized. Although the baby was born out of wedlock, Ellen feels it is her duty as a Southern lady to help those less fortunate than she.

8. Scarlett not only looks up to her mother but feels Ellen is actually a miracle: a source of comfort to all and capable of charming and soothing.

9. Scarlett doesn't know of her mother's great and lost love before accepting Gerald's proposal; nor does he, for that matter. All except Ellen thought she was being an obedient daughter in accepting Gerald's marriage proposal.

10. Gerald constantly shows his kind heart but is unaware that everyone else knows of it. He thinks yelling is a way to hide this but his actions belie the volume of his voice.

Chapters 3-5

New Characters:

Pork: *Gerald's body slave*

Dilcey: *Pork's wife*

Prissy: *Dilcey's daughter*

Suellen and Careen O'Hara: *Scarlett's two younger sisters*

Summary

After hastily emigrating from Ireland under dubious circumstances when he was 21, Gerald O'Hara, a man without fortune or education, won an impoverished Tara during a drunken poker game, making a reality of his ambition to own a plantation. Ten years later, realizing Tara needed a mistress and he a wife, he married Ellen Robillard, 28 years younger than he. She was from Savannah, where he had gone to ask his older brothers, James and Andrew, to help him find a wife.

After the death of her one true love, her cousin Philippe when she was 15, Ellen told her parents she would marry Gerald and move to Tara or join a convent. Along with Mammy and 20 house servants, Ellen became the able mistress of the plantation, the wonderful mother of three daughters (the three sons following died very young), and a good neighbor to all.

During a dinner at which Ellen is not presiding because she has taken Mammy with her to attend to their neighbor, Emmie Slattery's dying newborn bastard, Dilcey and her daughter, Prissy, arrive from Twelve Oaks and thank Gerald for buying them both. Pork, Gerald's valet, married Dilcey and this will allow the new family to live together at Tara.

Scarlett later overhears her mother demanding that her father dismiss their overseer, Jonas Wilkerson, and realizes he is the father of Emmie's child. While the younger O'Hara daughters adhere to the teachings of Ellen and Mammy as to becoming ladies, Scarlett is a tomboy.

As a young woman of sixteen, Scarlett refuses to accept Ashley's engagement to Melanie, convincing herself the engagement has happened only because Ashley does not know that she loves him. She proceeds to plan her elopement with him and spends most of the morning agonizing over how best to profit from her appearance and behavior while Mammy attempts to convince her to eat now (so she will not later in public) and cautions her about her choice of outfit.

On the way to the Wilkes' plantation with his daughters, Gerald encounters Mrs. Tarleton and her daughters. They stop to discuss the day's upcoming barbecue while Scarlett continues to secretly fantasize about her elopement with Ashley. Mrs. Tarleton speaks against Ashley's marriage to Melanie because she opposes marriage between relations; Melanie and Ashley are cousins. The conversation is terminated when the children urge their parents to proceed to the barbecue.

Analysis

While Ellen shows herself as a responsible, caring person by nursing Emmie Slattery and her dying babe, and Gerald unwittingly demonstrates his kindheartedness by purchasing not only Pork's new wife, Dilcey, from Twelve Oaks but also her daughter, Prissy, Scarlett proves her self-centeredness by refusing to accept Ashley's engagement. It is incomprehensible to her, despite Gerald's previous talk with her, that he would marry anyone else but her. While her younger sisters and the Tarleton sisters are busy contemplating the fun to be had at the barbecue and their parts in it, Scarlett is planning how she and Ashley will elope, possibly this same day. Mammy, who is very well aware of Scarlett's self-centeredness, wonders how Ellen could do such a good job of raising young ladies and yet have Scarlett, with her fairly obvious disregard for the norms of society, as her daughter.

Study Questions

1. Why did Ellen marry Gerald?

2. Why does Scarlett refuse to accept Ashley's engagement?

3. How did Gerald obtain Tara?

4. When do Dilcey and Prissy come to live at Tara?

5. Why is Mrs. Tarleton opposed to Ashley and Melanie's marriage?

6. When is Jonas Wilkerson dismissed?

7. How does Mammy know Scarlett is not a lady?

8. What does Scarlett plan to do at the barbecue?

9. Why is Ellen not presiding at dinner when Pork's new family arrives?

10. What is Scarlett's opinion of the Tarleton sisters?

Answers

1. When Ellen was a girl of 15 in Savannah, she was in love with her wild cousin, Philippe Robillard, but he was killed in a brawl in New Orleans. Wanting to leave her family and her memories of Philippe, Ellen accepted Gerald's proposal and agreed to move to Tara, vowing she would enter a convent if

her family attempted to prevent this marriage and her sub-
sequent move.

2. Scarlett has convinced herself that Ashley is marrying
    Melanie because he does not know Scarlett loves him.

3. Sitting in a saloon, Gerald overhears a stranger talk of his
    ruined plantation and arranges an introduction with the
    thought of winning this plantation in another drunken poker
    game. Betting with his brothers' money, he does just that.

4. Pork, Gerald's valet, married Dilcey who lived at Twelve Oaks
    along with her daughter, Prissy. When they married, Gerald
    went there to buy them both from their master, John Wilkes,
    at Pork's request so they could live with Pork at Tara as a fam-
    ily.

5. Mrs. Tarleton is opposed to marriage between relations.

6. Ellen implies to Gerald that Jonas Wilkerson is the father of
    Emmie Slattery's dead newborn baby. She demands that
    Gerald terminate the employment of Mr. Wilkerson as their
    overseer since he did not marry Emmie.

7.   Mammy knows Scarlett prefers "tomboy" activities and is
    not at all interested in education.

8. Scarlett plans to be gay and catch everyone's attention
    thereby proving she is not upset at Ashley's impending en-
    gagement.

9. Ellen has taken Mammy with her to attend Emmie Slattery's
    newborn baby who is dying.

10. Scarlett is both shocked and envious that the four Tarleton
    sisters treat their mother as they would a girlfriend.

Chapters 6 -7

New Characters:

Charles Hamilton: *Scarlett's first husband*

Rhett Butler: *a guest at the barbecue who watches Scarlett*

Ashley Wilkes: *a neighbor Scarlett convinces herself she is in love with*

Honey and India Wilkes: *Ashley's sisters*

Melanie Hamilton: *Charles' sister and future wife of Ashley*

Wade Hampton Hamilton: *Scarlett and Charles' son, born after Charles' death*

Summary

Scarlett, who has previously stolen Honey Wilkes' beau, Stuart Tarleton, begins flirting with Charles Hamilton, although he has an "understanding" with Honey. Rhett Butler watches Scarlett so boldly that she asks who he is, only to be told of his terrible reputation. Rhett once compromised a young lady by keeping her out quite late without a chaperone. Melanie and Ashley spend their time exclusively with each other at the barbecue while Gerald begins a heated discussion about war. Charles uses the subject to discover Scarlett's feelings for him, after which he declares his love for her and proposes. Rhett attempts to show the other men the lack of logic and common sense in the South's fighting a war but to no avail.

During the rest period between the barbecue in the afternoon and the ball at night, Scarlett sneaks out of the bedroom to find Ashley. She succeeds, declares her love, and horrifies Ashley. Unbeknownst to her, Rhett is in the room and hears the entire discussion. Upon returning to the bedroom, Scarlett hears the other girls describe her as "fast" with only Melanie saying a word in her defense. Just after, Charles announces that the war has begun and he will be leaving before the ball, as will the other volunteers. He extracts Scarlett's promise to marry him very soon.

Two weeks later, they marry on the day before Melanie and Ashley's wedding. Only six weeks later, Charles dies of pneumonia following measles while in camp in South Carolina. A bored, pregnant Scarlett becomes depressed with Charles dead and Ashley in the army.

Upon the birth of her son, Wade Hampton Hamilton, Doctor Fontaine, mistakenly thinking Scarlett is in deep mourning, suggests a change of scenery. Scarlett and Wade visit relatives in Savannah and Charleston but return with Scarlett in an even worse depression. Ellen, still thinking Scarlett's depression is the result of heartbreak over Charles' death, sends them to visit his aunt, Pittypat Hamilton, and her niece, Ashley's wife Melanie, in Atlanta.

Analysis

In these chapters Scarlett progresses from a narcissistic 16-year-old who attends barbecues and balls, flirts with every man (available or not), and is scorned by her female contemporaries as "fast" to a 17 year-old-widow with a baby who is thought to be in deep mourning. However, it is only society's view of her which changes; she is still egocentric. It is her boredom with the life of a widow in the country which is misconstrued as mourning. Her feeling for war is only that it confines her to the social life of a widow, takes Ashley from her, and affords her some modicum of activity once she reaches Atlanta.

The one person who seems to see her as she is, rather than as she is supposed to be according to society, is Rhett Butler. Although he is older than her, he both frightens and excites her with his clear vision. Her husband, Charles, was actually meant to be nothing more than a cause for jealousy on Ashley's part. She never intends a life with him and, never having thought about it, is surprised at his marital demands and at finding herself a mother.

Living with his sister and aunt in Atlanta, Scarlett begins to better understand, but not love, her late husband. She still has no great need to think for herself since, while Mammy stayed at Tara, Uncle Peter is here to tell her what to do and how to do it, Prissy takes charge of Wade (however poorly), and Uncle Henry attends to legal matters. Perhaps this is just as well since her only life decision so far was to marry Charles. Her delight in being active and sought after again, even if it is just on the hospital committees, overcomes her distaste for living with Ashley's wife and she stays indefinitely.

Study Questions

1. Who are the couples at the barbecue?

2. Why does Scarlett not stay with the other girls during the rest period between the barbecue and the ball?

3. What is Ashley's reaction when Scarlett proposes to him?

4. Why does Rhett Butler overhear the proposal?

5. When does Charles Hamilton die?

6. Why does Scarlett go visiting?

7. Why does Scarlett flirt with Charles Hamilton?

8. How does Melanie defend Scarlett when the other girls call her "fast"?

9. How did Rhett Butler earn his terrible reputation?

10. In what way does the start of the Civil War hasten Charles and Scarlett's marriage?

Answers

1. Honey Wilkes and Charles Hamilton are planning to wed, Carreen is besotted by Brent Tarleton, Ashley and Melanie will announce their engagement that night, India Wilkes still cares for Stuart Tarleton even though Scarlett has spirited him away, and Frank Kennedy is already showing his interest in Suellen.

2. The barbecue is already over and Ashley has paid no attention to Scarlett, so she feels she must seek him out privately.

3. Ashley meets her proposal with silence, then consternation .He attempts to make a joke of it, then asks her to pretend she'd never told him she loves him when he sees she is serious.

4. Rhett is taking his own nap on a sofa in the library, having already alienated the rest of the male guests with his talk against the South entering this war .

5. Charles joins the Wade Hampton Legion in South Carolina. There, before he ever gets to fight a single battle, he contracts measles. It is the pneumonia following the measles which kills him, only six weeks after his marriage to Scarlett.

6. After Charles' death and the birth of their son months later, Scarlett becomes thoroughly bored with being a young widowed mother in the country. Others misconstrue her behavior and think she is depressed. After trying all available remedies, Dr. Fontaine suggests to Ellen that Scarlett needs a change of scenery.

7. Scarlett cannot find Ashley, and is momentarily distracted by her first sight of Rhett. Seeing Stuart Tarleton in a mood to be difficult if she flirts, she does just that—with Charles Hamilton, Ashley's prospective brother-in-law.

8. Melanie seeing only the good in others, prefers to think of Scarlett has " . . . high-spirited and vivacious."

9. Rhett Butler has been disowned by his family for being expelled from West Point. He also took a lady for an unescorted buggy ride, and killed her brother who had challenged him to a duel to defend her honor.

10. Scarlett wishes to exact revenge on Ashley as soon as possible.

Suggested Essay Topics

1. Although Scarlett is now a 17-year-old widowed mother, her behavior is not much different than it was when she was a 16-year-old, childless, single Southern belle. How does this reflect both her lack of emotional growth and wartime mores?

2. How does Ellen's "treatment" of Gerald offer insight as to the traditional roles of male and female in the antebellum South?

3. Part I has introduced us to the different types of slaves and their positions in the family. Using specific characters, explain each different type of slave and what the expectations for this type of slave are.

SECTION THREE

Gone with the Wind, Part II

Chapters 8-10

New Characters:

Pittypat Hamilton: *Charles and Melanie's spinster aunt*

Uncle Peter: *Pittypat's slave*

Mrs. Elsing, Mrs. Merriwether, and Mrs. Whiting: *the leaders of Atlanta's society*

Henry Hamilton: *Pittypat's lawyer brother*

Summary

Uncle Peter, Pittypat's slave turned "keeper" who practically raised Melanie and Charles since they were orphaned very young and had Pittypat come to live with them, meets Scarlett, Wade, and Prissy (who comes along as the baby's nurse) at the train station, giving orders the second he lays eyes on them. Scarlett is surprised to see that Atlanta is no longer the little town she remembers, born only nine years later than she and christened the same year as she. Due to the war, Atlanta is now a busy, sprawling city with many hospitals and other wartime industries.

On their way to Pittypat's, Uncle Peter passes the leaders of Atlanta's society and Scarlett sees her first "bad" woman (without knowing what a "bad" woman is). Scarlett agrees to join a hospital committee and continues to greet those from Atlanta who had come to Tara for her wedding less than a year before. While Uncle Henry, Pittypat's lawyer brother, tries to explain the terms of Charles' will to her, Scarlett is too excited and happy to be in Atlanta to pay attention.

Having worked hard getting things ready for the bazaar, Scarlett resents not being able to attend since those in mourning were not expected. She sobs, but Pittypat and Melanie think her weeping is for Charles. Mrs. Elsing and Mrs. Merriwether arrive to plead for their help at the bazaar since several ladies have to cancel. Because the bazaar is to raise funds for the hospital, Pittypat reluctantly agrees when Scarlett says it is their duty to come out of mourning and help, although no one was suggesting that she, a widow of less than a year, make an appearance.

At the bazaar, Melanie loudly accuses the young men who are not in uniform of being cowards while Scarlett defends them, repeating what she's been told: they are needed to protect Atlanta. Melanie refuses to accept this but the argument is interrupted by Dr. Meade. As Scarlett struggles to contain her desire to dance, she spies Rhett Butler, now a blockade runner, and is afraid he will mention Ashley's rejection of her marriage proposal.

Rhett engages her in conversation, hearing the news of Charles and Ashley's fates for the first time. Then he teases her. Much as she feared him, she now finds herself enjoying his company. Dr. Meade requests all the ladies donate the jewelry they're wearing to the Confederate Cause. Scarlett gives her wedding ring which prompts Melanie to do the same. Rhett makes it clear he is aware of Scarlett's true motivation in doing so—to be free of the constant reminder of Charles—just as Dr. Meade an-

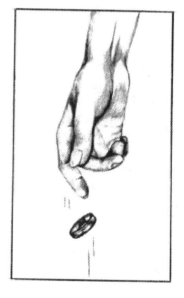

nounces an auction of dancing partners to raise even more funds for the hospital. Rhett successfully bids for Scarlett and she accepts, despite Dr. Meade's protests that she cannot dance while in mourning.

The next morning both Pittypat and Melanie are angry with Scarlett. She presents Rhett's idea of not staying home anymore since her reputation is already ruined as her own. Melanie comes to her defense, but Scarlett spurns her support. Melanie receives a package from Rhett containing her wedding ring which he redeemed for 10 times its worth in order to return it to her. Ellen sends a letter to Scarlett only three days later condemning her conduct at the bazaar and announcing Gerald's impending visit to Atlanta. Scarlett fears what her father will do, specifically that he may fulfill Ellen's threat of bringing her back to Tara.

Gerald arrives bringing the news that Joe Fontaine and Sally Munroe married, Stuart Tarleton is once again courting India Wilkes, and Brent Tarleton is openly expressing an interest in Carreen, Scarlett's youngest sister. When they are alone, he tells Scarlett he will be taking her back to Tara. But later, after a night of drunken poker playing with Rhett, Gerald must strike a bargain with Scarlett that he will not make her return if she does not tell Ellen of his drunkenness or poker losses.

Analysis

Scarlett's true colors—a vain, self-centered, willful girl—are beginning to become obvious. Her insinuating herself at the bazaar, her callous evaluations of the other young women, and her inability to comply with society's rigid behavior code lead her to honest self-evaluation. She is shocked to realize she is not only unpatriotic but incapable of loving to the extent she thinks other women do. As she struggles to find a way of living with this new knowledge of herself, Rhett—the one person who already knows this about her—appears.

This leads to her further confusion since he joins her in keeping this secret while pretending she is a lady. Her family and friends think her misconduct and moodiness is caused by Charles' death, but Rhett knows she is bored and angry with being denied pretty clothes, dances, and beaux. Gerald also has an inkling of the true

Scarlett but only as far as her selfishness with former beaux.

Rhett and Scarlett combine their wiles, although Scarlett is not certain that this is why Rhett gets Gerald drunk and helps him lose a large amount of money in a poker game, to force him into letting Scarlett stay in Atlanta. Ellen does not see her daughter for who she is and is dismayed by her conduct. Melanie, who is blinded by her love for Ashley, assumes Scarlett has the same sort of love for Charles and keeps defending her actions as those of a heartsick widow. Scarlett has no patience for this patent untruth but does not tell Melanie how wrong her perception is.

Study Questions

1. Why does Scarlett come out of mourning?
2. Why did Mrs. Elsing and Mrs. Merriwether not ask Scarlett to come out of mourning?
3. What are Scarlett and Melanie expected to do?
4. Why does Dr. Meade first interrupt the proceedings at the bazaar?
5. Why is Scarlett dismayed to see Rhett?
6. How does she scandalize society?
7. About what does Ellen write Scarlett?
8. How does Scarlett react when Melanie defends her?
9. About what does Gerald tell Scarlett?
10. Why does Scarlett not have to return to Tara?

Answers

1. A bazaar is being held to benefit the hospitals. Mrs. Bonnell was to manage a booth but her children have the measles. The McLures, who were also to help, have to go to Virginia to fetch their wounded brother. Mrs. Merriwether and Mrs. Elsing ask Pittypat and Melanie to take their places since the remaining young women will not tend the booths, preferring to dance and court. Scarlett uses the need for women to tend the booths as an excuse to come out of mourning.

2. Society's rigid code of behavior demands that widows not appear at social functions for at least a year.

3. The girls are expected only to manage a booth selling whatever goods the ladies of the town have made.

4. Dr. Meade announces that in order to raise more funds to buy medical supplies from England, the ladies are now going to be asked to donate whatever jewelry they are wearing to be melted down and sold.

5. When Scarlett first sees Rhett, not realizing who he is, she takes delight that a man is finally noticing her as something other than just a widow. Recognizing him, she is aghast remembering how he had witnessed Ashley reject her proposal and then Rhett's brutal honesty about the situation

6. Scarlett scandalizes society by accepting Rhett's bid for her partnership in the first reel as part of the auction.

7. When Ellen hears of Scarlett's behavior at the bazaar, she immediately writes to her censuring her dancing in public and her choice of partner.

8. Melanie misconstrues Scarlett's actions as those of a heartsick widow who is not thinking clearly. At this latest defense of her, Scarlett is self-centered enough to think, "You'd be glad to do without me if you knew what I really think of you."

9. Gerald tells Scarlett about her former beaux choosing other women. Scarlett is distressed, not willing to admit she has no claim to them. He reminds her that she is a widow and her recent conduct unacceptable.

10. Scarlett strikes a deal with Gerald to keep silent about activities if he agrees not to take her home in disgrace and promises to convince Ellen that Scarlett is the innocent victim of gossip.

Chapters 11-13

Summary

A tired Scarlett returns from the hospital and secretly reads Melanie's letters from Ashley. She is accustomed to doing so although she occasionally reminds herself that Ellen would not approve. She loses interest when she realizes Ashley is writing of possible defeat in the war. Scarlett is still convinced he loves her, but doesn't know why she cannot understand him—his way of thinking or his actions.

Despite the deprivations of wartime and still wearing black clothes, Scarlett is happy to be out of mourning. The informality of wartime also greatly relaxes the rigid societal code of behavior; not only is Scarlett done with her formal mourning before the proscribed time, but she behaves as a young girl would: flirting, riding, dancing, going to parties—yet still dressed in mourning clothes. She thinks of herself as a young belle despite having a child (who is being so well cared for that she almost forgets him). The one "fly in the ointment" for Scarlett is she misses her mother who is so busy with Tara's part in the war effort that she has little time to spare when Scarlett does visit.

Her most usual companion in Atlanta is Rhett. Her secret fears that he may betray her by revealing her thoughts and that she may be amusing to him make her hold her temper in check when she is with him, something she has done for only one other person before—Ellen. Yet she finds Rhett exciting, even though she knows she is not in love with him. Nor can Pittypat resist his little gifts and so allows his visits despite his less than complete acceptance by society and her own feeling that he has no respect for women.

Melanie, on the other hand, feels Rhett is a gentleman since he returns her wedding ring. She believes he only needs the love of a good woman to reform. Scarlett is quite irritated that Rhett treats Melanie so well when he has told Scarlett honestly in private that, yes, he is a rascal and, no, Scarlett is not a lady. Rhett is also immune to Scarlett's attempts to make him court her.

Mrs. Merriwether needs white satin for her daughter's wedding dress so Rhett, unbidden, brings it from England which

prompts her to invite him to dinner. Such acts and his knowledge of fashion, garnered on his business trips abroad, help to endear him to Atlanta's womenfolk. As the city's inhabitants begin to accept him, Scarlett finds her association with him becoming more acceptable. However, this is short lived and ends at Mrs. Elsing's silver musicale (which is organized to raise funds for the hospital) when Rhett begins to alienate these same people with his view that war is a "money squabble" rather than an expression of patriotism. Mrs. Merriwether admonishes both Pittypat and the young women, Scarlett and Melanie, to have nothing further to do with him. While Scarlett seethes in silence, Melanie openly refuses to terminate her friendship with Rhett and explains that Ashley has the same opinion of war, much to Mrs. Merriwether's shock.

Dr. Meade writes a letter to the newspaper protesting such sentiment. His letter is soon followed by others. As the blockade tightens, rumors begin to circulate that Rhett is the source of the rising prices and more dire scarcity of goods, causing his ostracism from all but one home, Pittypat's. This exception is made only because Melanie insists. Scarlett likes the little gifts Rhett brings when he visits, but also wants the gossip about Rhett to stop, so she attempts to convince him to keep his thoughts to himself and redeem himself by enlisting.

Rhett explains that England will never come to the South's aid (as is necessary for the South to win). He further explains that he was cast out of the social system she wants him to redeem himself with a long time ago because of his refusal to conform to a boring, Southern Charleston. Scarlett half agrees with his feelings but, cannot repudiate this Southern system herself, preferring to continue to wear black although that is her only concession to mourning.

Rhett brings her a colorful bonnet from Paris as a gift, but will allow her to keep it only if she promises not to turn it into a mourning garment. She agrees, thereby breaking another of society's rules: a lady may not accept expensive gifts from a gentleman. She thinks this is a step in courtship, but Rhett quickly negates the thought and warns her that he is a bad influence on her. She cannot see this.

The next day, Melanie runs in crying to tell Scarlett she was speaking with Belle Watling and doesn't want Pittypat to know. Belle wants to help in the hospital but Mrs. Elsing will have nothing to do with Belle since she is a prostitute, so Belle seeks Melanie in order to donate $50 in gold. Belle requests that she be allowed to continue her anonymous donations every week. As she is speaking to Melanie, Uncle Peter drives up and yells at Melanie. Now Melanie begs Scarlett to convince him to say nothing to Pittypat, but Scarlett is distracted by the handkerchief in which Belle wrapped the money for it has the initials R.K.B. on it. She realizes Belle and Rhett are in some way involved.

Analysis

Scarlett unconsciously continues her inner struggle to behave like a lady and yet fulfill her own desires. She does not know why it is so easy for her to read Melanie's letters, re-enter society while in mourning, or accept Rhett's gift, but, though she knows Ellen would not approve. Rhett, in his honesty, explains why the war is not a noble cause and why society has no attraction for him.

Scarlett continues to prove herself self-centered as she accepts Rhett's gift of a colorful bonnet although she continues to wear mourning clothes. She seems afraid to totally break with society's dictates, but her selfishness is stronger than her fear. She thinks Mrs. Merriwether wrong to censure Rhett, but does not protest, fearing to do so would hurt her own position. She secretly searches Ashley's letters to Melanie for indications he loves her, yet she completely misses his direct statements about the war's probable outcome. Lastly, when she sees the handkerchief with Rhett's initials in which Belle wrapped the money for the hospital, her first thought is only that this is proof Rhett could not love her.

Study Questions

1. What is Scarlett searching for as she secretly reads Ashley's letters?

2. How does Rhett initially gain acceptance in Atlanta's society?

3. What does Mrs. Merriwether admonish Pittypat, Melanie, and Scarlett to do?

4. Why does Melanie refuse to do as Mrs. Merriwether demands?

5. Why does Dr. Meade write a letter to the newspaper?

6. What does Scarlett attempt to persuade Rhett to do?

7. Why does Rhett bring Scarlett the colorful bonnet from Paris?

8. Why does Melanie ask Scarlett to intercede on her behalf?

9. Why does Belle Watling speak with Melanie?

10. Why is Scarlett outraged that the handkerchief Belle tied the money in has Rhett's initials on it?

Answers

1. She is still searching for evidence that Ashley is in love with her but doesn't know it.

2. Because of his trips to Europe for the Confederate Cause, Rhett is in a position to see the new fashions and takes careful note of them to relate to the ladies in Atlanta.

3. Mrs. Merriwether admonishes Pittypat, Scarlett, and Melanie to stop receiving Rhett.

4. She feels it unjust to bar Rhett from their home since, although the words are different, Ashley and Rhett's sentiments are the same.

5. Without naming Rhett, Dr. Meade writes a letter to the newspaper against speculators, profiteers, and holders of government contracts. He insinuates Rhett is a blockade runner purely for his own financial gain.

6. Scarlett asks Rhett to think what he will, but to keep these thoughts to himself, which is her own system for acceptance. Rhett refuses to be a party to such hypocrisy.

7. He knows Scarlett's mourning is insincere and so brings the bonnet, but will not allow her to have it unless she promises not to drape it with mourning. He is tempting her to break with society even more.

8. Uncle Peter sees Melanie speaking to Belle Watling, a pros-

titute, in public outside the hospital. Losing all sense of propriety, he—a slave—yells at his mistress and proceeds to scold her all the way home. Melanie is afraid he will tell Pittypat and so, upon arriving home, begs Scarlett to help her convince him not to.

9. Belle Watling wants to help the Confederate Cause. She asks Melanie to take her donation but to keep its source anonymous, fearing it won't be accepted if Mrs. Elsing knows it is money earned through prostitution.

10. Scarlett is outraged when she sees that the handkerchief Belle tied the money in has Rhett's initials because, to her, it means he couldn't possibly love her.

Chapters 14-16

Summary

Although the South continues to believe in its eventual victory, letters begin to trickle home from the soldiers asking for boots and supplies. News arrives of the fall of Vicksburgh to the west as Lee fights in Pennsylvania. Pittypat, Melanie, and Scarlett join the others at the offices of the newspaper to get news of Ashley.

Rhett joins them, announcing the first casualty lists have been sent to the newspapers and are being printed. He fights the crowd to bring them the first galley proofs. Ashley's name is not on the casualty list, although the following are: Dallas McLure; Darcy Meade; Raiford Calvert; Joe Fontaine; LaFayette Munroe; and Brent, Stuart, and Thomas Tarleton. Rhett leaves to tell Dr. Meade of his son's death and Scarlett takes the emotionally exhausted Pittypat home to put her to bed.

Afterward, as Melanie and Scarlett sit with Mrs. Meade awaiting the doctor's arrival, Phil (the Meade's younger son), makes it clear he wants to join the army, although his parents will not allow it. Melanie tells Scarlett how jealous she is that Scarlett has Charles' child, both for having a baby and for having a part of Charles which remains after his death.

A haunted Ashley comes home on leave. Scarlett is frightened

by how much she loves him. Arriving four days before Christmas, he brings the drunken Fontaine boys with him to await their own train home. After the emotional greetings, Scarlett begins to plot once again how to convince Ashley that he loves her. Yet later, it suddenly dawns on Scarlett, when Melanie and Ashley go into their room closing the door behind them, that he is indeed Melanie's husband, not hers as she wants him to be.

The week passes swiftly. When it is time for Ashley to leave, she gives him her going away present of a silk sash she made herself and promises to do anything for him. He asks her to look after Melly for him and admits he's been lying all week about the South's winning. At her request, he kisses Scarlett goodbye. She attempts to turn this into a passionate kiss and confesses her love for him. With mixed emotions, Ashley leaves.

While Scarlett purposely misunderstands Ashley's mixed emotions to her advantage and plans how they will be together after the war, Melanie announces her pregnancy. Scarlett now knows for certain that Melanie and Ashley have been having sexual relations and feels like a wife with an unfaithful husband. She plans to leave the next day rather than stay in the same house with Melanie, but they receive a telegram that Ashley is missing in action and believed killed. Scarlett and Melanie take whatever comfort they can from each other.

Days later, Melanie faints in public and is brought home by Rhett who offers to use his influence in Washington, D.C., to obtain information about Ashley. He discovers Ashley is wounded and a prisoner in Rock Island, Illinois, one of the worst provisioned and most impoverished Yankee camps. The Northern President Lincoln halts all prisoner exchanges. It comes to light that Ashley had been offered an exchange before the halt and had refused it because it would have meant taking an oath of allegiance to the North and spending two years fighting Indians in the West.

Analysis

The South, except for the soldiers who keep silent in order to protect those at home from even more worry, is slow to realize how poor its position is geographically, economically, and strategically. It is only through the requests the soldiers send home for clothing and provisions, plus their manic behavior when they do get leave, that the people at home begin to suspect the South is not winning, although they will not admit they are losing. The casualty lists are long and devastating. Scarlett loses most of her childhood friends and recent beaux to the war, but is obsessed only with Ashley's welfare.

Despite Melanie's talk of having Ashley's baby, Scarlett immediately resumes her plotting when Ashley comes home on leave. Even seeing them together for the whole week does not convince her to stop. She is self-involved, seeing the world as she wants it to be—until it occurs to her that Melanie and Ashley must be having sexual relations behind the door they close to the rest of the world every night. Having had limited, uninspired experiences herself, and only with Charles, she is repelled and fascinated at the thought.

Rhett once again shows his respect for Melanie by being the first to get the casualty list and giving it directly to her, rescuing her when she faints in public, and offering to use his influence to find the whereabouts of her husband. Rhett is beginning to emerge as a courageous man, not without principles, but rather with a set of his own making which seem superior to those of society or Scarlett.

Study Questions

1. When do the Southerners begin to suspect they are not winning the war?

2. Why do the people gather at the newspaper office?

3. Why is Melanie jealous of Scarlett?

4. Why does Ashley bring the Fontaine boys home on their layover between trains?

5. Why is Scarlett angry Melanie is giving Ashley a coat for Christmas?

6. How does Scarlett confound Ashley when she catches him alone just before he leaves?

7. How does Scarlett feel when Melanie announces her pregnancy?

8. Why does Scarlett not leave Atlanta as she had planned?

9. What information about Ashley does Rhett discover when he uses his influence?

10. Why does Ashley refuse to take part in a prisoner exchange?

Answers

1. Soldiers are sending home letters asking for boots and explaining how they have to loot both corn from the farmers' fields and pieces of uniforms from dead Yankees and each other.

2. A crowd is gathering in front of the "Daily Examiner" because the newspapers will be printing the first casualty lists.

3. Melanie is jealous of Scarlett because she has Charles' child. Melly is afraid Ashley will be killed in the war and she will not have the comfort of having a child of his to live on after his death.

4. The Fontaine boys are drunk and aggressive. There is a two hour wait at Atlanta before their train arrives and the others are having a hard time keeping these boys from fighting.

5. Scarlett still harbors the illusion that Ashley loves her. She wants to be able to give him such a personal gift, but this is the sort of gift a wife gives a husband.

6. For the second time, Scarlett declares her love for Ashley, but not until she asks him for a farewell kiss and hug which she attempts to turn into a passionate embrace. He disentangles himself from her embrace and leaves.

7. Scarlett feels as if Ashley is an unfaithful husband to her. She is surprised that he has sexual relations with Melanie since she feels he loves her (Scarlett), not his wife.

8. Scarlett does not leave as she had planned because they receive a telegram from Mose, Ashley's body servant, saying he cannot find Ashley; in other words, Ashley is missing in action.

9. Ashley is a prisoner in Rock Island, the worst prisoner of war camp, located in Illinois.

10. Ashley refuses to take part in a prisoner exchange (before they are halted) because it would require an oath of allegiance to the North and then enlisting for Indian service in the West for two years.

Suggested Essay Topics

1. When Scarlett arrives in Atlanta, she sees a very different place than the small town she remembers. How is the city different and how did these changes come about?

2. The Southern ritual of mourning is rigidly proscribed. In what ways does Scarlett adhere to this ritual and in what ways does she not?

3. The Confederacy is often described as waging "total war" against the Union, due to the people's unending support, loyalty, and contribution. How does this apply to Melanie and Pittypat's social circle when Scarlett stays with them?

Gone with the Wind, Part III

Chapters 17-18

Summary

While the people of Atlanta assure themselves the Confederacy will not allow this all important city to be attacked, Mrs. Meade worries that her younger son, Phil, will have to fight; the wounded Captain Ashburn realizes his courtship of Scarlett is not progressing; Rhett and Wade continue developing a fondness for each other; and Pittypat has a dinner party to share the last remaining fowl— a rooster. Rhett arrives uninvited, despite the hard feelings the other guests have for him, and is reluctantly invited to stay.

As the enemy attacks closer to home, at New Hope Church, the homes of Atlanta are flooded with wounded since the hospitals become overloaded. Pittypat protests when it is her turn to house the wounded since she feels it is unseemly to have strange males in the house when Melanie is so obviously pregnant, but Melly insists.

Scarlett lies to Mrs. Merriwether, telling her Ellen needs her at Tara, but Mrs. Merriwether says she will write to Ellen to say how much more Scarlett is needed in Atlanta. Scarlett runs away from the hospital feeling she cannot stand it any longer, but runs directly into Rhett, who looks well-fed, clean, and stylish, much to Scarlett's chagrin.

He explains how close the enemy really is—in the Kennesaw

Mountains, only 22 miles away. As Atlanta becomes aware of the sounds of cannon, the Home Guard, including Phil Meade, marches out. Ashley's body servant, Mose, appears acting as John Wilkes' servant. John soon appears himself, riding Mrs. Tarleton's horse Nellie, and with messages from home for Scarlett. She is concerned with her status in the courtship competition since she is aware that, as a widow of 19 with a child, she is not as appealing as an unmarried 16-year-old childless woman; there are many of these in Atlanta during the war. With the help of the cloth Rhett brings her for pretty clothes, she manages to socialize nightly, while marriages become a daily occurrence due to the haste caused by war.

During the battle of Atlanta, the ladies watch the fighting from the rooftops as they shade themselves with parasols. It soon becomes apparent this is dangerous and the exodus to Macon begins. Mrs. Merriwether, Mrs. Elsing, and Mrs. Meade remain. Melly begs Scarlett to stay with her since Dr. Meade thinks the trains are unsafe for Melanie during her pregnancy and there is no doctor in the country to assist with the birth. Dr. Meade explains to Scarlett in private that Melly will have a difficult delivery due to her build and will need Scarlett, not the flighty Pittypat, to help. Pittypat goes to Macon as planned while Scarlett, reminded of her pledge to Ashley, stays in Atlanta with Melanie.

Analysis

The people of Atlanta are either unaware or unwilling to admit how close the battle is to home. It is only when the battle is actually in Atlanta that their exodus begins.

Scarlett still lives in her strange reality of nightly parties and daily nursing. Even as her current beau is killed, she is concerned with her chances of remaining part of courting. She barely acknowledges the existence of her son, Wade, although this little child is frightened by the blood and cries of the wounded. She leaves his rearing to Prissy, barely conceding his relationship with Rhett. She thinks only of herself, wanting to return to Tara to escape what she considers her odious duties at the hospital. Scarlett actually walks out when her help is so desperately needed and lies to Mrs. Merriwether in her efforts to flee from this obligation.

Rhett, as the realist, warns her of her need for loving and maturity as well as the seriousness of their situation as residents of Atlanta, but she once again sees this as nothing more than his amusing himself at her expense. For the first time, Melanie asks Scarlett for something—to keep her promise to Ashley to watch over Melly. Surprisingly, Scarlett bows to Melly's request and the pressure from Dr. Meade to stay in Atlanta with Melanie until the baby is born.

Study Questions

1. What is the path of the battles as they come closer to Atlanta?

2. Why does Pittypat have a dinner party?

3. Why is Rhett unwelcome at social events?

4. What is Scarlett's main concern before the battle of Atlanta?

5. Why does Pittypat protest having the overflow wounded from the hospital in her home?

6. Why is Big Sam in Atlanta?

7. When does the exodus begin?

8. Why do Mrs. Merriwether, Mrs. Elsing, and Mrs. Meade not leave?

9. Why does Melly stay in Atlanta?

10. Why does Scarlett, in turn, stay?

Answers

1. As Part III of the book begins, the Yankee army is above Dalton, 100 miles northwest of Atlanta, near the Tennessee line and begins to push the Confederate troops 65 miles back, closer to Atlanta at New Hope Church.

2. Because of the blockades, supplies are severely limited. Pittypat is worried because the pregnant Melanie has not had chicken in weeks since they have already eaten them all, so she decides to slaughter her sole remaining rooster.

3. Rhett alienates the Confederates by being realistic about their dire position in the war.

4. Scarlett worries that 19 is an advanced age for courting.

5. Melanie is now five months pregnant. Pittypat feels it is inappropriate for strange men to see her in this condition and, even more, is afraid that seeing some of the more badly wounded may cause Melanie to enter labor prematurely.

6. Since the Yankee Army is only 22 miles away in the Kennesaw Mountains, the Confederate Army decides to dig more rifle pits in more distant circles around Atlanta to prevent the Yankees from getting any closer. There is no available manpower so the strongest slaves from the plantations—Tara included—are impressed for this job. Gerald offers the services of Big Sam (their foreman), Elijah, Apostle, and Prophet.

7. The ladies of Atlanta take parasols with them to sit on the rooftops and watch the battle. As shells drop, they realize the immediate danger, hide in the cellars, and flee once night falls.

8. Mrs. Merriwether and Mrs. Elsing feel they are needed at the hospital and are unafraid, but they do send their daughters to Macon. Mrs. Meade defies her husband's orders to leave for two reasons: firstly, she feels the doctor needs her, and secondly, she wants to be near Phil, her younger and only surviving child, who is in the trenches.

9. Melanie feels she will be lonely without Scarlett and wants her there when the baby is born. Scarlett refuses to go to Macon to stay with Pittypat's cousin, Mrs. Burr, because she had called Scarlett "fast" during Scarlett's last visit.

10. Scarlett stays because Melanie reminds her of her promise to Ashley that she will watch out for Melanie and also because Dr. Meade explains to her privately that Melanie cannot give birth without a doctor's help.

Chapters 19-22

Summary

Scarlett is terrified as shells burst overhead and Melanie's due date draws near. Prissy assures Scarlett she can manage the birth since her mother is a midwife. Scarlett longs to go home but doesn't, only because of her promise to Ashley. She finds Wade troublesome in his fear and plans to have Prissy deliver him to Tara, then return to Atlanta in time for the birth but travel becomes too dangerous. As she becomes jaded by the terrible living conditions in a city under siege, she also becomes accustomed to soldiers knocking at the door for food, medical treatment, or a place to sleep.

Uncle Henry, on the way to protect Jonesboro, stops to say goodbye and asks Scarlett to inform Melanie her father-in-law is dead. As Uncle Henry fears, Jonesboro (which is only five miles from Tara) falls. Gerald writes of the battle and includes the information that Carreen, Scarlett's youngest sister, has typhoid. As Scarlett sits alone, thinking of her dead beaux, Rhett appears, aghast that Melanie is still in Atlanta and Scarlett with her. While freely admitting to herself she doesn't love him, Scarlett wants Rhett to love her. He tells her he doesn't, but wants her to be his mistress. She is indignant and orders him to leave.

Thirty days after the siege begins, the bombardment simply stops. General Sherman is striking at Jonesboro again as a way to get into Atlanta. A courier brings Scarlett news from her father: Suellen, Carreen, and Ellen all have typhoid now and she is to stay away. With the telegraph lines down and the mail disrupted, no one knows what is really happening.

Scarlett is torn wanting to be with her mother and knowing she has to be with Melanie. She awakes one morning to hear a cannon—from the south where Jonesboro and Tara are. Melanie tells Scarlett she knows Scarlett would go home if it were not for her and asks Scarlett to take her baby if she dies. Scarlett promises to do so when she sees Melanie will not stop asking until she agrees to her request. Melly tells Scarlett she is in labor but asks for Mrs. Meade since labor takes so long and the wounded have the greater need of Dr. Meade's services.

Prissy returns alone from going to fetch Mrs. Meade. Phil

Meade is wounded and his mother has gone to get him. Mrs. Elsing is occupied with the numerous wounded at the hospital so Prissy is sent for Dr. Meade. Yet again, Prissy returns alone, explaining that no one is available at the hospital. This time, Scarlett leaves Prissy with Melanie while she goes to find help. She passes people preparing to leave and learns Jonesboro is lost and the army, in preparation for evacuation, is opening the commissary warehouses. At the depot, she sees wounded and dying men all around her, begging for water. She approaches Dr. Meade who sends her to find his wife, not knowing that their son is wounded and that Mrs. Meade has gone to him.

Realizing Dr. Meade cannot come, Scarlett hurries home to find Wade hungry, Prissy frightened, and Melly in hard labor. Prissy admits she knows nothing about midwifery, causing Scarlett to strike her in anger. During Melly's labor in the sweltering heat, Scarlett alternately wishes herself dead or at home. Wade is minded by Prissy while Scarlett devotes herself solely to Melanie. Scarlett, terribly frightened for Melanie when she becomes weaker, sends Prissy to simply ask for directions from the Meades, but they are unavailable for Phil has died of his wounds. When Melly gathers from Prissy's babblings that the Yankees are coming, she tells Scarlett to take Wade and go, but Scarlett refuses.

The next morning, while Melly and her newborn son sleep, Scarlett sees the evacuating Confederate troops who tell her the Yankees are coming. She sends Prissy to tell Rhett to bring a horse and carriage to take them all from Atlanta.

Analysis

Scarlett is beginning to mature. While she desperately wants to see her ill mother and both give comfort to and receive comfort from her, she respects her pledge to Ashley and stays with Melanie. This is difficult for her and she constantly seeks solace and complains—but only to herself.

She finally understands that Melanie can be nothing but good (when Melanie asks her to send for Mrs., rather than Dr., Meade) and begins to accept this although it still puzzles her. She silently laments that there is no help now, becoming aware that she has always had someone to assist her whenever she's needed it. While she does not seem to appreciate this, she does recognize its absence. Even as she feels unequal to the task of attending Melanie in childbirth, she does not shirk this responsibility. It is a momentary attempt to "stand on her own two feet" and she succeeds, although she calls for Rhett's help very soon afterward.

Melanie is consistent in her goodness, thinking it obvious that wounded soldiers have more priority with doctors than a woman giving birth. The only sign of selfishness we see is when Wade cries for his mother but Melly begs her not to leave, and this occurs while Melly is practically delirious. It is becoming evident that Wade is what we now call a neglected child. His mother barely acknowledges his existence; Prissy, who is to rear him, is not quite out of childhood herself and extremely irresponsible; and Melanie, who dotes on him, is so badly frightened herself right now that she takes whatever little attention his mother would give him.

Study Questions

1. Why does Scarlett want to go home?
2. What are Scarlett's plans for Wade?
3. Why does Prissy tell her not to worry?
4. Why does Uncle Henry visit?
5. What does Rhett ask Scarlett to do?
6. When news does a courier bring from Gerald?
7. When does Scarlett strike Prissy?
8. Why is it that Dr. and Mrs. Meade cannot attend to Melanie?
9. What does Melanie ask Scarlett to do?
10. Why does Scarlett send for Rhett after the birth?

Answers

1. Scarlett is afraid; there are wounded and dying soldiers everywhere and they constantly stop at the house to ask for aid, food, and sleeping space.
2. Scarlet plans to send Wade with Prissy, then have Prissy return before the birth of Melanie's baby. She simply wants

Wade out of her way but the roads become too dangerous to implement her plan.

3. Prissy tells Scarlett not to worry because her mother is a midwife and Prissy has watched her at work many times, learning her skills.

4. Uncle Henry, as a member of the Confederate Army, is on his way to Jonesboro to help protect the railroad there so that the Yankees cannot use this area as an entry into Atlanta.

5. Rhett asks Scarlett to be his mistress, explaining he doesn't want to marry and has waited a long time to declare himself to her.

6. The news is that Ellen and both of Scarlett's sisters, Carreen and Suellen, now have typhoid. Ellen does not want Scarlett nor Wade to come home where they will be exposed to this dreaded disease.

7. Prissy admits she know nothing about midwifery. Scarlett strikes Prissy in anger at her lies.

8. Dr. Meade is at the depot attending the wounded who are arriving quickly and in great numbers. Mrs. Meade has been informed her son, Phil, is wounded and goes to bring him home.

9. Melanie is terrified of childbirth and has already asked Scarlett to take her baby if she dies.

10. Scarlett wants Rhett to bring a horse and carriage and take all of them away from Atlanta.

Chapters 23-25

Summary

Scarlett sits, waiting for Rhett to come take them away from the hell Atlanta has become. She sees flames and thinks the Yankees have come and are burning the city. Prissy returns and tells her it is their own soldiers who are doing the burning and that she

saw Rhett, who told her his horse and carriage were already commandeered, but he promises to get a horse. Scarlett tells Prissy to prepare Wade and the baby to leave. She has not been able to bring herself to go to Melanie since the birth of the baby. Rhett arrives and argues with her that she cannot go home as she wants to; the road to Tara is unsafe, but she becomes hysterical insisting she will and Rhett concedes. He bundles them all into the rickety wagon he's found. The only things they take are the daguerreotypes of Charles and his saber.

They ride through Atlanta, avoiding fire at every turn. Just before they come along the rear guard of the retreating Confederate troops, Rhett tries to give Scarlett a pistol to protect the wagon but she already has Charles'. Rhett maneuvers them safely through the city and makes certain Scarlett knows another, less dangerous road to lead them to Tara. He then tells her he's leaving them—he has enlisted and must join his troop. At first, Scarlett thinks he is joking; then she takes it as a personal affront. After giving Scarlett a passionate kiss farewell, Rhett leaves.

Melanie faints before Rhett leaves. Scarlett does not rouse her as they must spend a harrowing night on their journey and it will be easier for her to be unconscious. They have no food, no water, and lose their way many times before they finally unharness the horse (when he can go no further without some rest) and sleep in the wagon. In the morning, Scarlett is delighted to see they spent the remainder of the night under the Mallory trees, close to Tara, but her mood quickly changes when she sees the Mallory house is burned down and no one is there. Throughout their journey, they see dead men and animals. Melanie has no milk so when they finally spy a cow, they take her to feed the baby. Scarlett begins to fear Tara may also be burned down and her mother dead, but she tries to ignore these fears.

Tara is still standing when they reach it. Gerald is there but he is now an old man. He tells Melanie Twelve Oaks is burned. Pork arrives and takes Melanie in hand while Prissy brings the children inside. In response to her questions about the family, Scarlett is told by her father that the girls are recovering but Ellen died just the day before Scarlett arrived. Scarlett is in shock but still notices how dark the house is. She learns the Yankees took all the candles

but one, and the slaves, except for Pork, Dilcey, and Mammy, have
run off. Furthermore, apart from the forgotten yams and some
buried apples, there is no food.

The only good news is that Dilcey has just had a baby and can
serve as wet-nurse to Melanie's baby. Gerald explains that Tara
wasn't burned because the Yankees used it as headquarters and it
was a Yankee doctor who saved Carreen and Suellen from typhoid.
Scarlett purposely inebriates herself and her father. When she
checks her sisters, Mammy comes in, thankful that Scarlett is home
and will take responsibility for the household and tells her of Ellen's
death.

The next morning Scarlett faces the fact that her father is not
mentally functional and blames it on the shock of her mother's
death. She begins to manage the plantations once she admits to
herself her father will be no help. The slaves demure, saying they
are house servants and should not be doing the work of field hands
but she demands their obedience. Scarlett herself goes to Twelve
Oaks and finds vegetables. She vows never to be hungry again. Now
home at Tara, she is responsible for everyone and they all com-
plain about the lack of adequate food, with the usual exception of
Melanie.

Scarlett notices Wade is avoiding her but is too busy to deter-
mine why. Melly tries to intervene but is still weak. Scarlett bullies
the others into taking an active part in their own survival and, as
she does, confronts the thought that nothing she has been taught
as a young lady is of any help now. She resolves to keep Tara intact
as the family plantation.

Analysis

Scarlett is forced into full blown adulthood now. Rhett is not
there to take responsibility; Gerald is barely functional; Mammy is
not trained to think in ways that will guarantee survival; and her
sisters are weak from being ill and too "ladylike" to work. While
Scarlett alienates all those for whom she is responsible with her
bullying, she does succeed in forcing them to accomplish the ev-
eryday tasks necessary to ensure their survival.

There is food, even if the quality and quantity do not please the family. She allocates work and makes certain it is done, while she, herself, does more than her fair share of physical labor. Her resolve never to go hungry again assures that everyone at Tara will eat.

She is vaguely aware of a problem with her son but is still too frightened, too uncomfortable with the responsibility thrust upon her without warning to take the time to attend to him. Luckily for him, although she is still weak from the complications of child-birth, Melanie—in her innate goodness—reaches out to offer him whatever comfort she can.

As Mammy offers Scarlett the same admonitions to behave in a ladylike fashion, Scarlett is perplexed. These admonitions force her to concede that nothing her mother taught her is of help now, but Scarlett cannot understand why. She still has not come to see that war changes the world.

Study Questions

1. Why does Scarlett think the Yankees have arrived?

2. What is it Rhett manages to bring?

3. When does Rhett leave them?

4. What do they discover when they wake up?

5. How is Gerald different?

6. Why does Mammy not take responsibility for the family as Scarlett had hoped she would?

7. Why is Dilcey able to nurse Melanie's baby?

8. Why are Suellen and Carreen not much help?

9. How does Wade begin to act?

10. Of what does the food at Tara consist?

Answers

1. Scarlett sees the flames and light from the burning of sup-plies by the Confederates. In anticipation of evacuating At-lanta, and not wanting to leave anything the Yankees can use, the rear guard of the Confederate troops empties the com-

missary warehouses, then sets fire to them, the foundry, and the supply depots.

2. Rhett manages to bring only an old rickety wagon and a near dead horse.

3. Rhett leaves them only after conducting Melanie, Prissy, Scarlett, Wade, and the newborn baby safely through the fires and the drunken mobs.

4. They wake to find they are at the Mallory place near Tara but no one is there and the house is burned down. While there is water, there are only a few mostly rotten apples left.

5. When Scarlett sees her father, her first thought is that he is an old man. Later, when she becomes inebriated with him, she hears herself telling him what to do as one does with a child. He is nonfunctional as the head of the household.

6. Without Ellen, Mammy is a working lump of misery. She effectively nurses the girls through typhoid but has no idea what is necessary in a wartime world.

7. Dilcey and Pork have also had a baby. While Pork delicately questions why Melanie's baby needs cow's milk, Scarlett bluntly tells him Melanie is not producing milk for her baby.

8. When Scarlett arrives at Tara, Suellen and Carreen are still suffering from typhoid.

9. Wade is frightened of his mother. She never has time for him except to bark reprimands at him and has no understanding of how deep his fear is.

10. When Scarlett returns to Tara, she forces the slaves to remember food they have forgotten by questioning them.

Chapters 26-28

New Character:

Beau Wilkes: *Ashley and Melanie's only child*

Summary

Two weeks have passed. Scarlett knows Gerald lives in his own world. She plans to walk to Jonesboro to locate food, but her foot is infected and the horse is dead. When she sees a Yankee approaching the house, she sneaks the pistol from the drawer, hides it in the folds of her skirt, and kills him with it. Melanie lies to the others and mops the blood while Scarlett drags the body out of the house and buries it. Melly suggests they go through his knapsack and pockets where they find money and jewelry. They keep his horse.

Sally Fontaine arrives at Tara to warn them Yankees are coming again. Scarlett hides the pigs in the swamp, the food in the woods, the silver in the well, and has Pork hide Gerald. Melanie is told to take the horse and hide the cow and her calf in the swamp while Scarlett hides the money and jewelry in Beau's diaper. Deciding she cannot let the Yankees burn Tara, she sends Wade to find his aunt in the swamp and goes to meet the Yankees. Wade refuses to go, silently clinging to her skirts as the Yankees ransack the house, take the jewels they see, kill the sow, and set fire to the cotton. As they attempt to take Charles' sword, Wade sobs that it is his and the soldiers leave it for him after some squabbling. One of the soldiers, upset at leaving the sword, sets the kitchen afire. Scarlett cannot extinguish the fire herself. Melanie returns and helps her.

The cold arrives. With it come the realizations that they have no cotton or food and that their money is of little use because there is nothing available to buy. Fairhill, the Tarleton home, is burned down, as is the Munroe house.

Frank Kennedy visits to seek food for the commissary department which immediately causes Suellen to perk up. This is Christmas Eve, so all the women try to make it as festive as possible (under the dire conditions) for the soldiers. At the same time, ironically, they hide their little store of food so the soldiers will not take it.

The residents are beginning to return and rebuild, living in tents, shacks, or log cabins until their new homes are ready. Savannah is lost and the Yankees have started using military academy cadets and convicts to fill their ranks. Frank asks Scarlett for permission to marry Suellen, which surprises her, since she thought he had asked Gerald years ago.

Analysis

As conditions go from bad to worse, Scarlett accepts her role as head of the house but feels so unsure of herself, so trapped without solutions, that she begins to have nightmares. Her respect for Melanie, albeit begrudging, continues to grow as she finds Melly there whenever she is needed, uncomplainingly performing distressing but necessary acts without qualms, even cleaning up after a murder, attempting to pick cotton, or hiding animals from soldiers.

Only Dilcey silently obeys Scarlett's every order with the attitude (which is shared by Melly) that Scarlett is in charge and the physical strength Melly does not have. Scarlett's sisters are weak and while Carreen tries, she cannot meet the physical demands of labor. Scarlett realizes she's never liked Suellen but knows she is still responsible for her. After browbeating everyone into doing their share for the family's survival, Scarlett is left alone—a terrified woman spontaneously doing whatever is necessary and pushing her limits to keep them all from starving.

She knows, unequivocally, that she must succeed. She must find food, even if it means allowing Pork to steal and hiding whatever they have from her own army. She commits murder to save Tara. Her love of Tara and the cotton increases dramatically as she struggles to save them. It seems the less food there is and the more hopeless the struggle to find some, the greater her focus on this love of the land and its crop. Before the war and the hardship it brought, she couldn't be bothered to talk with Gerald about her inheriting Tara, nor even consider for herself what that might mean. Now thoughts of Tara and the cotton consume whatever energy remains in her after the struggle to feed everyone.

Study Questions

1. When does Scarlett commit murder?
2. What do Scarlett and Melanie find in the thief-soldier's pockets?
3. What is Grandma Fontaine's advice to Scarlett?
4. What do the Yankees do the second time they come to Tara?
5. How is Beau instrumental in the family's survival this time?
6. Why do the soldiers leave Charles' sword?
7. Why does Frank Kennedy come to Tara?
8. What does he tell them about Atlanta?
9. What does Frank ask Scarlett?
10. Why do the women try to make it a lively evening for the soldiers?

Answers

1. Scarlett is alone when she hears a horse. Seeing it is a Yankee cavalryman, she rushes into the house for her pistol. He comes in, unaware that she is there, and begins to steal whatever he can carry. He hears her and she shoots, killing him in cold blood.

2. Before Scarlett drags the body out to bury it, Melly suggests they search it. Scarlett finds a wallet stuffed with money in his pocket and many kinds of gold, silver, and jewels in his knapsack.

3. Grandma Fontaine advises Scarlett to pick her own cotton rather than let it rot. When she learns of Ellen's death and Gerald's mental infirmity, the old woman advises her to save some fear for it's unnatural for a woman not to fear.

4. This time, Sally Fontaine warns them of the approach of a group of Yankees. The warning affords the family time to hide most of the food and animals and get Gerald away. The soldiers still pillage as much as they can and one sets fire to the kitchen.

5. Scarlett hides a wallet full of money in Beau's diaper. It is this money which will be used for food as long as any is available.

6. When the soldiers try to take Charles' sword, Wade stops them, prompting Scarlett to protest to the sergeant. Despite its solid gold hilt, the sergeant (who was at the same Mexican War battle where Charles' father was awarded the sword) agrees to let Wade keep it.

7. Frank Kennedy is now on a mission for the commissary department of the Confederate Army to find food for the troops.

8. Frank relays the news that Atlanta is now being held by the Confederacy again.

9. Frank Kennedy wants to marry Suellen. He plans to ask Gerald for permission but when he sees Gerald's mental condition, asks Scarlett as head of the house instead.

10. It is Christmas Eve and each of these soldiers, except for Frank, has been physically maimed by the war. Their appreciation for simply being near pretty women and sleeping on a rug in a house endears them to the family.

Chapters 29-30

New Character:

Will Benteen: *Confederate soldier left at Tara to recover from pneumonia*

Summary

General Johnston surrenders and the war ends. Pork spends five weeks on the road returning with clothes, seeds, and food. Scarlett is glad of the war's end, thinking it will be the end of her fear. Suellen and Scarlett fight over the horse; Suellen wants to make use of him for social visits while Scarlett insists he is only for work. The argument ends when Scarlett slaps Suellen.

Scarlett continues as head of the house, buying seed, oversee-

ing the planting, supervising the daily household tasks, and making sure there is food.

The Confederate soldiers begin to return home. All are lice-ridden and infected with dysentery. Mammy doses them with a blackberry root concoction to help with the dysentery, bathes them, and washes their clothes before she allows them in the house. Scarlett turns the parlor into a dormitory for them. When the soldiers have no news of Ashley, the family reminds Melanie that if he dies, a priest will write a letter home and because they haven't received one, he must not be dead.

Uncle Peter comes to Tara with Pittypat's pleas for Melanie and Scarlett to return to Atlanta. He and Mammy argue about where the girls are needed most, much to the family's amusement. He gives Melanie a letter from Ashley which arrived in Atlanta. She promptly faints. While she is unconscious, Scarlett reads the letter. Ashley is coming home.

Will Benteen arrives, so ill with pneumonia they expect him to die. Carreen spends a great deal of time nursing him and even more praying for her dead love, Brent Tarleton. Will is good at listening so the family talks to him, individually, of their hardships and woes. As soon as he is able, Will begins to help in the house and with the children. He asks to stay. He is welcomed and soon becomes indispensable. He is good with animals, a shrewd trader, and a hard worker despite his convalescence and wooden leg. He slowly becomes a member of the family. Scarlett sees he cares for Carreen, but Carreen does not.

Ashley arrives. As Melanie runs to meet him, so does Scarlett. Will stops her by holding her so she cannot reach Ashley. He reminds her that Ashley is Melanie's husband, not hers.

Analysis

The war ends but Scarlett, having changed throughout it, knows her responsibility as head of the house is not over. Food is still her primary concern. She is delighted Pork is able to save some of the money she'd given him to buy supplies. She thinks Melly will be a charity case on her hands for the rest of her life and is perturbed that Melly suggests Cathleen live with them, to provide her dying brother some comfort, rather than marry Mr. Hilton. Scarlett sees only another mouth to feed. She begrudges the returning soldiers every mouthful they eat. She has matured, and in so doing, has become hard. She thinks of herself much as a modern business woman does, but in terms of her capacity to produce food, rather than dollars.

There is still a streak of self-centeredness in Scarlett. When she discusses the lack of men for Southern women to marry, it is in the back of her mind that this may affect her at some time in the future. While Carreen is mourning the death of Brent, she thinks it would be one less mouth for her to feed if only Carreen would marry Will. While Rhett admires her frankness and is amused at her egocentric thoughts, Will sees her clearly and tries to put an end to her interfering with Ashley. Rhett talks while Will acts, holding her back when Ashley returns home.

Study Questions

1. Where is Pork sent?

2. Over what do Suellen and Scarlett fight?

3. When do the Fontaine brothers become angry?

4. Why does Mrs. Calvert praise Mr. Hilton?

5. Why is Cathleen Calvert going to marry Mr. Hilton?

6. What does Carreen ask Beatrice Tarleton to do?

7. What is the condition of the returning Confederate soldiers?

8. Why does Uncle Peter come to Tara?

9. Who is Will Benteen?

10. What effect does Ashley's arrival have on Scarlett?

Answers

1. Pork is sent to Macon to buy cotton and garden seed.

2. Never having walked anywhere before, Suellen thinks she needs the horse to go visiting. Scarlett maintains the horse is for work and must rest when not working. The argument ends when Scarlett slaps Suellen.

3. Scarlett goes to Mimosa to buy corn seed. The Fontaine boys agree but then will not accept the money. There is a certain amount of pride still left in Alex and Tony (who never plowed or farmed before) and Scarlett, unwittingly, injures it.

4. Mrs. Calvert is a Yankee who came south when she married 20 years ago. She is constantly making social blunders since she does not understand Southern ways. Mr. Hilton is her husband's overseer and also a Yankee. By telling this to the Yankee soldiers, the burning of their house was averted twice. Both Cathleen and Cade, the children of her Southern husband by his first wife, are terribly embarrassed that this is what saved their home.

5. Cade Calvert, Cathleen's brother, is dying. Her Yankee stepmother, the second Mrs. Calvert, is taking her four young daughters north permanently. Their overseer, the Yankee Mr. Hilton, is willing to marry Cathleen.

6. She wants to see her family's tombstones and asks Beatrice to take her there.

7. The soldiers are full of lice and dysentery. They are hungry, ragged, and have little strength.

8. Pittypat returns to Atlanta from Macon and is afraid to be alone. She sends Uncle Peter to Tara to bring Melanie and Scarlett.

9. Will Benteen is a returning Confederate soldier who is so ill from pneumonia when he reaches Tara that no one expects him to live.

10. Ashley's arrival throws Scarlett into confusion once again.

Suggested Essay Topics

1. The Civil War overturned the traditional roles of male and female, parent and child, master and slave. How is this evidenced in this novel?

2. Rhett and Ashley are usually considered opposites; however, there is a great deal of material in the story which strongly

suggests they have more in common than is suspected. Analyze each of these characters to find and explain these similarities.

3. At the end of the Civil War, the South was in a ravished state—this is what Tara looked like to Scarlett when they finally reached there after fleeing Atlanta. What changes were there in the great plantations due to the war and how did each of these changes happen?

Gone with the Wind, Part IV

Chapters 31-32

Summary

Part IV of the novel begins as Scarlett writes to Pittypat, once again, to explain why Melanie, she, and now Ashley, cannot return to Atlanta. Will enters her office to talk about the taxes which are being raised by the new Reconstructionist government since someone, possibly Mr. Hilton, wants to buy Tara and thinks he can do so at a sheriff's sale if the new, much higher taxes cannot be paid. Scarlett finds this incomprehensible, so Will explains that Scalawags and Carpetbaggers are really in charge now, along with the garrisoned soldiers and those running the Freedmen's Bureau, who just happen to be their former overseer, Jonas Wilkerson, and his assistant, Mr. Hilton.

Scarlett looks for Ashley in the orchard, saying she needs his advice but really looking for a private moment with him. He suggests going to Rhett but Scarlett discounts that idea. He tells her he is a coward, afraid of this new life, and she argues this is not so. He speaks in flowery terms she does not understand but he does kiss her palms. She urges him to run away with her, but Ashley insists he doesn't love her and cannot possibly leave Melanie or Beau; he reminds her of her responsibility to her father and sisters.

When she begins crying, he kisses her then breaks from her

embrace saying the embrace is his fault, not hers, and he will leave with his wife and child. But first, Ashley admits he does love her. Scarlett thinks the world is over for her, but he reminds her how much she loves Tara. She suddenly understands his honor prevents him from coming with her and tells him he and his family need not leave Tara.

Scarlett acknowledges Tara is all she has left just as Jonas Wilkerson arrives with his wife, the former Emmie Slattery. Both look quite prosperous. Scarlett orders them away, but Jonas will not go until he threatens to buy Tara out from under her. Scarlett is afraid there is some truth in this threat unless she can find the $300 for the new taxes. Knowing a loan for this year will not take care of the future, she resolves to marry Rhett (despite her hatred for him) and never have to worry about the taxes again. She remembers he said he's not the marrying kind and decides, if she cannot be his wife, she'll accept his offer to make her his mistress. Her conscience bothers her just a little, but she reminds herself she has nothing left to fear, so why not gain security this way?

She plans to seduce him into remembering his offer but worries that she is no longer pretty enough and has Mammy make her a new dress from the green, velvet curtains. Mammy has her suspicions and plans to go to Atlanta with Scarlett. Both Will and Ashley have their own suspicions, but feel helpless to stop her.

Analysis

Scarlett no longer has any vestiges of the young Southern belle left in her. Her belief that peace or Ashley would save her is shattered. She crystallizes into a hard realist, knowing she can rely only on herself to save Tara. She has little compunction about taking up Rhett's offer now; Scarlett only regrets that he is the one to be their salvation. She thinks she hates him for the very thing she feels will save them—his offer to make her his mistress. Scarlett sees nothing amiss in her contradictory feelings because she doesn't analyze them; she sees the need for quick money, a way to get it, and proceeds.

Her dream of being with Ashley is gone, for the time being. She kissed him when he was home on leave; he kisses her now and admits his desire and love for her but, because of honor and loyalty, will not act upon them. Scarlett hates and admires this in him. As the grown-up she's been forced to become by the war, she thinks she relinquishes her dreams of Ashley, yet tells him he and his family do not have to leave Tara. His honor prevents him from speaking to Scarlett when he suspects she is going to Atlanta to get Rhett's money but not by borrowing it.

Nor has the end of the war saved her. In her naivete and immaturity, she thought it would, but there is still the struggle for food and now, money, as the interim government makes a mockery of the tax structure. She doesn't care what happens to the rest of the South, just Tara. It is only when Tara is threatened by these new "leaders" that Scarlett becomes aware of their tactics, and even their existence. She sees Tara as an extension of herself now, so it is included in her self-centeredness.

Her thoughts for the rest of the world go only so far as she and Tara need them to in order to survive.

Study Questions

1. Why does Scarlett not go back to Atlanta?
2. How does Ashley spend his time?
3. About what does Will tell Scarlett?
4. For what purpose does he think the taxes are being raised?
5. What does Ashley tell Scarlett?
6. What does Scarlett understand about Ashley?
7. What does she plan to do first?
8. What does Scarlett ask Mammy to do?
9. What does Scarlett remember about Rhett's feelings for her?
10. Why is Mammy going to Atlanta with Scarlett?

Answers

1. Scarlett is still needed as the head of the house. While she has Will to share the responsibility, she is the decision-maker and supervisor since he is not family.

2. Ashley is trying to be a farmer, to do his share of whatever is necessary on the plantation.

3. He explains that the taxes on Tara will be assessed at an additional $300.

4. Will believes that Hilton wants Tara for himself. The two men have the power to raise the taxes so high that Scarlett would not be able to pay them. Tara would then be offered at a sheriff's sale and Hilton could buy it.

5. When they are alone in the orchard, Ashley tells Scarlett he loves her but cannot act upon his feelings.

6. Scarlett understands Ashley's honor will not allow him to leave Melanie and Beau; his loyalty will keep him at Tara but away from Scarlett.

7. At first, Scarlett plans to borrow the money using the diamond earbobs as collateral or sell them to him outright, but soon realizes this is a temporary reprieve from the taxes and she wants more permanent security.

8. In order to seduce Rhett, Scarlett feels she needs to be prettier or have prettier clothes. She asks Mammy to make her a petticoat from the satin lining of the green moss curtains.

9. Scarlett remembers Rhett doesn't want to marry but only to have her as his mistress.

10. Mammy is suspicious that Scarlett wants a new dress just to arrange a loan.

Chapters 33-34

Summary

The next day, Mammy and Scarlett arrive unannounced in a still-ruined Atlanta. They see rebuilding all around them but most of the shops bear names they do not know. Scarlett is disturbed by the number of Yankee soldiers. Belle Watling passes, obviously prosperous. The Meade and Whiting homes are gone. The Elsing's is

being repaired, as is the Bonnell's, but Mammy and Scarlett do not see the families.

Scarlett presses Pittypat for information. She learns Pittypat's farms, town property, and money are gone. Even the house she lives in really belongs to Melanie and Scarlett, and Uncle Henry is having trouble keeping the taxes paid on that. Scarlett knows he also saved one piece of downtown property for Wade and her. Pittypat tells her of neighbors renting rooms to other neighbors and of people doing whatever menial jobs they can to make money. Finally, she brings the conversation around to Rhett.

He is in jail for killing a freed slave who insulted a white woman. It is possible he may hang but the case still needs to be proved. Pittypat thinks the Yankees may make an example of him in retaliation for Ku Klux Klan activity but, then again, maybe they will not since he has millions in gold belonging to the Confederacy hidden somewhere—possibly in English banks.

The Yankees insist this money now belongs to them, but Rhett is not telling where it is. Scarlett has visions of marrying him quickly and his being hanged just as quickly, after he tells her where the money is. Mammy interrupts to suggest bedtime and Scarlett tells Pittypat she has an incipient cold and will stay in bed all the next day.

In the morning, after listening to make sure everyone else (except Cookie who will not be leaving) has left, Scarlett starts to walk to the firehouse which is being used as a jail. She gets a ride from a woman who thinks she is a hussy. The sentry at the jail is overcome by the tears he thinks Scarlett is going to shed when he begins to tell her visitors are not encouraged. He has another soldier take her to the captain, who remarks Rhett has many sisters when Scarlett announces she is Rhett's sister who has come to see him. She turns to leave in anger but yet another soldier detains her, saying Rhett refused to see yesterday's "sister."

Rhett appears, excited to see her. The officers give them privacy in the orderly room, where Scarlett almost convinces Rhett she is truly upset at his imprisonment, until he sees how coarse her hands are. He quickly surmises this is all a show because she wants something—money. She offers herself as his mistress but he cannot accept. Rhett cannot reach the money without the Yankee soldiers confiscating it. Scarlett's anger is out of control at this news and the soldiers, hearing it, rush in. Rhett and she convince them she fainted and they leave the room. He wryly tries to advise her on her seduction technique, but she refuses to listen.

Analysis

Scarlett forgets that Rhett is like her: cold, hard, and calculating. It is those parts of him he sees reflected in her that attract him. While he is initially drawn into her deception, he does not accept that she loves and cares for him. In her self-focus, now extended to include Tara, she has no compunction about lying to Pittypat and Mammy, nor sneaking out to the jail. She uses her wiles to gain entry to Rhett and lies boldfaced about the depth of her feelings for him. What makes this very clear to the reader is her momentary vision of marrying him, obtaining his money, then seeing him hanged for the murder of the freed slave. She has no compassion for his plight, just hope of saving Tara.

Her anger when she learns he has no access to the money, contains no thought for him—only despair at the loss of what she considers her last hope. Once she no longer needs to pretend any emotion for Rhett, she feels some—utter hatred. Apparently, he is no longer of any use to her.

Study Questions

1. When they arrive in Atlanta, what do Mammy and Scarlett see?

2. What does Scarlett learn from Pittypat?

3. Why is Rhett in jail?

4. How does Scarlett lie to Mammy and Pittypat?

5. Why does Scarlett sneak out?

6. How does she gain entry to the jail?

7. Why does Rhett not refuse to see her?

8. What does she pretend to feel?

9. How does Rhett know Scarlett is lying?

10. When does she allow him to see her hatred for him?

Answers

1. Much of the town is still destroyed but there is furious building and repairing happening. There are Yankee soldiers everywhere and freed slaves are driving carriages for hire.

2. Pittypat tells Scarlett that Rhett Butler is in jail.

3. Rhett is seemingly in jail for the murder of a freed slave who insulted a white woman. However, there is no proof of his guilt as yet so the town surmises he is going to be hung in retaliation for Ku Klux Klan activity—in other words, he is going to be the sacrificial lamb.

4. Scarlett tells them she has a cold, and plans to stay in bed all day.

5. She sneaks out to the firehouse (which is being used as a jail by the Yankees) to see Rhett.

6. The first sentry is just about to refuse Scarlett's request to see a prisoner when he thinks she starts to cry. He quickly calls another sentry to take her to headquarters. She goes in and asks for the captain, who is amused that another "sister" of Rhett's shows up. Scarlett angrily turns to leave but a younger officer detains her, saying Rhett refused to see yesterday's visitor but he will bring her name to Rhett now.

7. Scarlett is the first respectable visitor he has had and he is lonely. He thinks her visit means she has forgiven him for leaving her outside a burning Atlanta to get Melanie, Beau, Prissy, Wade and herself to Tara without his help.

8. Scarlett pretends she is doing well and that Tara has become prosperous. She also pretends her visit is solely for the purpose of telling Rhett she's worried about him.

9. Rhett knows Scarlett is lying when he kisses one of her hands while pressing the other against his cheek. He looks at this hand before kissing it and sees it clearly. Rhett knows these are the hands of a laborer, not a lady.

10. Rhett tells Scarlett he cannot give her the money because he cannot get to it. She wants to kill him, but faints instead. When she regains consciousness, she tells Rhett she hates him.

Chapters 35-36

Summary

A dejected Scarlett walks back to Pittypat's house, encountering Frank Kennedy along the way. He gives her a ride in his buggy and she looks at him anew. He asks about Suellen and tells Scarlett he's settled in Atlanta now and has a moneymaking store here. He also tells her of the sawmill he wants to buy. He's saving his money to marry Suellen so Scarlett knows he won't lend her any if she asks. She resolves to marry him herself for his money.

She fabricates a story about going to Yankee headquarters to see if she could sell the soldiers some fancy work for their wives. She plays on his sympathies, flirting with him and asking him what she should do to earn money. She lies to Frank, telling him Suellen is going to marry Tony Fontaine. Mammy sees them coming home together and thinks Scarlett came to Atlanta to see Frank. She tells her she's relieved because, while Rhett may have money, Frank is a gentleman. Mammy tells Scarlett she will help her win Frank.

Frank escorts them to Fanny Elsing's wedding that night where Scarlett is welcomed warmly. Rene Picard, now married to Maybelle Merriwether, teases her about being a widow so long and she, nastily, teases him about delivering pies, but he just laughs. She declines to dance saying she's still in mourning for her mother and spends the time comparing the room with what it had been before the war. Just being at the wedding, hearing the music and jokes, makes her feel the changes the war has caused even more strongly. She thinks of the changes within her, but they puzzle her except that she knows for certain she doesn't feel like a lady and is ashamed to be poor. She decides it is worth marrying Frank to save Tara.

Two weeks later, Frank and Scarlett marry. During the courtship, he answers her questions about his business while Scarlett pretends not to understand the explanations. Scarlett insists the marriage ceremony be a private affair with no family or friends and only strangers for witnesses. He gives her the money for the taxes even though it means he cannot buy the sawmill immediately. She continues to pander to him. While Atlanta is their permanent home now, Scarlett wonders what Ashley thinks of her and this marriage, even as she receives a scathing letter from Suellen. The people of Atlanta gossip but that has no effect on Scarlett. Frank comes to understand that Scarlett is an astute businesswoman and is interested in his shop.

Frank realizes, when Tony Fontaine comes to Atlanta on business and his own sister in Jonesboro writes to him, that Suellen never intended another marriage and he has jilted her. This means the whole town—and more importantly, he—knows Scarlett trapped him into marriage with her lies. He does not insult her by asking the truth of this; he is a loyal husband.

Frank develops the grippe and Scarlett offers to put his mind to rest by stopping in at his store. While there, she checks his account books. It suddenly occurs to her that she could do a better job of managing his business than he does. Rhett comes in while she's at the shop and insinuates she married for convenience. Rhett tells her he blackmailed someone in Washington to be released, yet admits his guilt and that in another murder, too. He tells her the money was in Liverpool and she should have waited for him instead of rushing into another marriage. Once again, he calls her on her hypocrisy and forces her to see the truth about herself.

Rhett offers her a purely business transaction: a loan to purchase the sawmill but only in return for the right to discuss Ashley with her whenever he wants. He insists Ashley in not interested in her mind but has carnal thoughts about her. She is abashed and protective of Ashley which makes Rhett think she's a fool. He makes her think about this and she doesn't want to.

Scarlett requests that Rhett come to the mill with her, right then, in the rain, before someone else buys it or Frank learns of her intentions. She tells Frank she sold Rhett her diamond earbobs to raise the money to buy the mill and operates it herself with only Uncle Peter to protect her. She also peddles the lumber in town herself and people are talking (again). Her mill is succeeding.

She sends most of the money, with directions for its use, to

Will Benteen at Tara. She talks to the embarrassed Frank of her plans to branch out into other businesses. He is sorely perplexed by the difference between this woman and the one he thought he married. Scarlett begins to show her temper when her judgment is questioned. Frank takes refuge in his store; only Mammy can withstand these outbursts. Scarlett no longer has any respect for Frank as a husband or a businessman. She feels he does not want her to be good at business. He thinks a baby will make her happy and keep her close to home.

Analysis

Scarlett is determined to do anything to save Tara. Her last hope—Rhett's money—is dashed. She is fighting for her existence and clutching at straws; the nearest one is Frank Kennedy, her sister Suellen's fiance. He mentioned the magic word—money. She is willing to forego living at Tara, her sister's bonhomie, gossip in Atlanta, Rhett's jeers, Mammy's suspicions-turned support: anything to save Tara, and she does.

Not only does she see the stopgap measure of paying the taxes when Frank mentions the money he's saving to marry Suellen, but she hears a permanent reprieve when he mentions the sawmill he intends to buy.

Yes, she will be providing for Ashley, Melanie, Beau, Gerald, Wade, Suellen, Carreen, Will, Pork, Dilcey, Prissy, and Mammy as well as herself but, she thinks only in terms of herself and her love for Tara. Since Tara is now an extension of herself, by saving Tara Scarlett is saving herself. She does not see that she is sentencing herself to a life in Atlanta, her new husband's home, among people who disdain her.

As usual, Rhett is the one to speak truthfully to her about her motives for marrying again, her willingness to sell her body if necessary, and her disregard for other people. Although she is married to Frank, there is a very clear triangle here with Rhett being truth, Ashley some vision of Scarlett's making, and Scarlett herself recognizing Rhett's truths but unwilling to give up her fantasy version of Ashley.

Study Questions

1. Why does Scarlett lie to Frank about why she was at Yankee headquarters?

2. What does Frank tell her?

3. Why does Scarlett resolve to marry Frank?

4. Why does Mammy offer to help Scarlett win Frank?

5. When does Frank realize Scarlett trapped him into marriage?

6. When Frank has the grippe, what does Scarlett discover by going to the store?

7. What does she realize?

8. What does Rhett admit?

9. How does Rhett explain Ashley's feelings for Scarlett?

10. What does Rhett agree to do?

Answers

1. Scarlett tells Frank the lie because she knows his opinion of Rhett is very low. She also wants him to think the situation at Tara even worse than it is.

2. In the course of their conversation, Frank tells Scarlett he went into active service soon after he'd been to Tara for the commissary department and was wounded. After the war, he saw all the hospital equipment piled along the railroad tracks by the retreating Confederate soldiers who didn't have time to burn them as they'd planned so the Yankees couldn't make use of them. He collects these goods and resells them cheaply.

3. Scarlett needs Frank's money. She feels she must save Tara and Rhett has just told her he cannot help.

4. Mammy thought, correctly, that Scarlett's coming to Atlanta for the tax money would involve Rhett somehow. She feels that Frank may not be good looking, but he is a gentleman, something Rhett definitely is not.

5. Scarlett said Suellen planned to marry Tony Fontaine, but he comes to Atlanta on business obviously still a single man

6. Scarlett discovers Frank is not a very good businessman. The store itself is dimly lit, with no system in the storeroom, and dirty. His account books tell her he has many, too many, accounts receivable open.

7. Scarlett is stunned to realize she can manage Frank's store better than he does.

8. Rhett admits he killed the man he was accused of murdering and another besides, a Yankee cavalryman he had words with in a barroom. In addition, the Confederacy's money was in a bank in Liverpool under his name. He arranged for his own release by blackmailing someone in Washington, threatening to name all the Yankees who sold him bullets and machinery during the war unless he gains his release.

9. Scarlett has a romantic vision of Ashley as her soulmate. Rhett, forever the realist, forces her to see (in her own mind if not publicly) that Ashley only lusts for her.

10. Rhett agrees to lend Scarlett the money to purchase the sawmill in exchange for the right to discuss Ashley with her whenever he chooses. He is willing to forego interest on the loan if she accepts this condition.

Chapters 37-38

Summary

Tony Fontaine arrives in Atlanta on a dark and stormy night, requesting help. He has killed Jonas Wilkerson, Tara's former overseer, and needs money and a horse to flee. Wilkerson filled freedmen's heads with the right to accost white women. While drunk, one of them caused Tony's sister-in-law, Sally, to scream in fright. Tony shot him and went after Wilkerson.

Ashley met Tony on the way to Jonesboro to kill Wilkerson and wanted to do it himself because of the way Wilkerson acted about Tara, but Tony insisted he must do it. Ashley held back the others while Tony told Wilkerson why he was killing him and knifed him to death. Now Tony must flee to Texas.

Frank hints that such people are being tended to when Scarlett expresses her dismay at being able to do nothing to protect her own kind from freed slaves and Reconstructionists. He doesn't tell her what is being done but says regaining the vote will finally rectify life for Southerners. In response to this lecture, she tells him she is pregnant.

Soldiers search their house again and again. Scarlett does not understand how Ashley could send Tony to them and hates Tony for bringing these searches upon them. She realizes the only rights existent in the South belong to the freed slaves and the Yankees. Everyone and everything else is regulated, including the newspapers and how or why a Southerner can be brought into court.

Former slaves are told they are free—then left to die of sickness, starvation, or drunkenness. The Ku Klux Klan arises in an attempt to contain the hordes of "mean niggers" or those simply doing whatever they can for their own self-preservation (since they have not been taught responsibility or right from wrong). There are also many white drunks, gamblers, thieves, and pickpockets with so many saloons opening and the houses of vice blooming.

Supposedly, Rhett gives Belle Watling the money to buy her own house of prostitution with a barroom on the ground level. Scarlett is afraid, but it is not just physical fear. She worries about what could happen if she has to start her business over again and pushes herself to succeed quickly. She knows how easy it is for the new government to jail her and is very careful to cause no offense and stay to herself. She has to stop working soon because of her pregnancy.

She nags Frank into making the store do better and collecting some bills. She now has competition from other sawmills but is still doing well. She uses both her ladylike airs and cold business manner, whichever works, to further her business. She lies about, and undersells, her competitors. After her first business lie, she never again thinks of what Ellen's opinion of her business affairs would be if she were still alive.

Scarlett drives the one competitor who tells the truth, that she is a liar and a swindler, out of business. Then she buys his sawmill.

Now she needs a manager, but not an unscrupulous one like Mr. Johnson at her first sawmill. She asks several of the young men who have their own, somewhat menial, businesses but they all refuse, preferring to work for themselves than for a woman. Tommy Wellburn suggests a Carpetbagger or Hugh Elsing, his brother-in-law. Scarlett reluctantly hires Hugh for his honesty but thinks he is stupid.

Frank supports the family in Atlanta while Scarlett sends half the money she makes to Will, gives part to Rhett to repay the loan, and hoards the rest. She fears losing her money and tries to carry as much of it as possible on her person. She is trying desperately to get her affairs in order before her pregnancy causes her retirement.

Scarlett begins to socialize with Yankees. She still hates them but knows she needs their business. She preys on their loneliness. The Scalawags and Carpetbaggers also begin to patronize her sawmill, preferring her graciousness to the cold courtesy of the other Southerners. Because of her, they patronize Frank's store as well. The Yankee women want her company, but ask her ridiculous questions about slaves. She is not happy to spend time with them and is outraged by their bigotry and ignorance. She leaves in a huff when one of them insults Uncle Peter, but he is hurt that she doesn't speak up in his behalf and will no longer drive her.

Rhett no longer calls at the house but accidentally meets her on her business route often. As her pregnancy progresses and the tensions in town mount, these meetings occur more frequently. He tells her she is not liked because she's different and successful in the ways she is different. She does a man's job which affronts the men, leading to her continued loneliness. Rhett inadvertently admits he's been watching over her because of her pregnancy.

He cautions her it is not safe for her to ride alone, and if she is raped and the Klan responds, the Yankees will enforce even more regulations and penalties on the townspeople. He also tells her she must get a more manageable horse so she will have more control; this one may bolt and overturn the wagon harming her and the baby.

Scarlett begins to drink, something decent women do not do. She uses brandy to relax, to sleep, to try to dull the ache in her heart for Tara and Ashley. She plans to go home when the baby is born but goes earlier when she receives a message that Gerald is dead.

Analysis

Further demonstrating her egocentricity, Scarlett drives her wagon by herself after Uncle Peter refuses to be seen with her in public. The horse is balky and difficult to command. Once again, Rhett—the realist, points out to her that not only must she be tired after trying to control the horse but that this is a dangerous practice; if the horse bolts, the wagon could overturn harming the baby as well as her. On a more civic level, it's downright thoughtless. Should a drunken freed slave accost her and succeed in raping her, the men in Atlanta will feel they have no alternative but to lynch him. That, in turn, will cause the Yankees to censure them even more stringently. In a sense, Scarlett could be responsible for the deaths of her neighbors through her inability to see beyond her own desires.

Rhett shows a side of himself that has only been hinted at before. He is a realist; now it is apparent that is the cause of his love of babies and children. He feels they are still innocent enough to be honest—no hypocrisy, no lies, just who they are. Perhaps this is part of the reason he admires Scarlett for her frankness and self-centeredness; it is childlike, although she successfully does a man's job.

Frank surprisingly shows strength and determination when Tony Fontaine comes to his door in the middle of the night after committing a murder. While Scarlett needs answers, Frank asks no questions but quickly and firmly gets Tony what he needs—a coat, some food, a horse, and some money. He apparently has more knowledge of what's happening in the South than he's let Scarlett know. This is another aspect of the older, sickly storekeeper who lets his wife nag him into a successful business and throw temper tantrums at home.

Study Questions

1. Why does Tony Fontaine arrive, unannounced, in the middle of the night?

2. When does Scarlett tell Frank she is pregnant?

3. Why are the former slaves not succeeding in their new lives?

4. Why does Scarlett push herself to succeed quickly?

5. Why does she have trouble hiring a manager for the second sawmill?

6. Why does Scarlett begin socializing with Yankees?

7. Why doesn't she care for their wives?

8. Why does Uncle Peter refuse to drive for Scarlett?

9. Why does Rhett take to "accidentally" meeting Scarlett on her business route?

10. What does he ask her to do?

Answers

1. Tony Fontaine kills Jonas Wilkerson in a knife fight. He is now fleeing to Texas and needs money, a horse, a coat, and food—quickly and quietly. Ashley tells him to go to Scarlett's house in Atlanta for the things he needs.

2. After Tony leaves, Frank tells Scarlett this reign of terror and fear will end when every Southern man can vote. She doesn't understand when he explains. He finishes by saying it may not even happen until the next generation. It is then that she abruptly tells him she's pregnant.

3. The former slaves are handed their freedom and their rights but they receive no counsel on what to do with them.

4. At the time of the novel, as soon as women become pregnant, they shut themselves in their houses for propriety's sake. Scarlett continues working far past the acceptable point but even she knows she won't be able to go out in public much longer and she is desperate, not only to get her affairs in order, but also to earn and save every single dollar she possibly can while she can.

5. The men of Atlanta do not want to work for a woman.

6. Yankees are good for business. Not knowing how long they'll

be stationed in Atlanta, they are building homes and sending for their families.

7. Scarlett finds the Yankee wives bigoted and lacking intelligence.

8. After Uncle Peter is insulted by a Yankee woman, he tells Scarlett he has back pains and can no longer drive her.

9. Rhett is concerned for Scarlett. He knows she's pregnant, driving herself, and blind to the dangers of her actions.

10. Rhett asks Scarlett to get a horse she can manage rather than risk having the horse overturn the buggy and hurt her or the baby.

Chapters 39-42

New Character:

Archie: *a murderer freed from prison for agreeing to fight in the Confederate Army*

Summary

Scarlett returns to a devastated Jonesboro wearing Mrs. Meade's ill-fitting black dress. Will is not there to meet her train, but Alex Fontaine goes to fetch him from the blacksmith shop. Thinking she already knows how Gerald died, Alex castigates Suellen to Scarlett before he goes. Will greets her warmly and asks for permission to marry Suellen, explaining Carreen will never recover from Brent's death and is planning to enter a convent. He tells her he decided the only way to stay at Tara, with Gerald dead and both Carreen and Scarlett living elsewhere, is to marry Suellen for propriety's sake. When asked, he confesses that Ashley, Melanie, and Beau are going to New York, where Ashley will work in a bank.

She immediately connives to keep Ashley in Georgia by making him the manager of her second mill. She begins crying when her thoughts turn to Gerald. That's when Will tells her Suellen was going to turn in a claim for property damage caused during the war by finagling the mentally murky Gerald into signing an Iron

Clad Oath swearing he was a Union sympathizer during the war. His mind cleared at the last minute and he refused to sign so Suellen tried to get him drunk in order to get him to sign. She almost succeeded, but once again, he refused to sign at the last minute. He grabbed a horse and was killed when he drunkenly attempted to jump fences, as he had done for Ellen before the war. The horse threw him and he died of a broken neck.

After a night's sleep, Scarlett's heart swells with pride as she sees how well Will has done for Tara. The neighbors are hostile to Suellen at the funeral. Ashley conducts the services, skipping the prayers about Purgatory Carreen marked for him, since he knows the neighbors will not understand them. The women intend to chastise Suellen for her part in her father's death, but when Ashley asks who will speak, Will quickly begins by announcing his engagement to her in an attempt to keep them from doing so. He doesn't want to have to respond in kind.

The people are confused, knowing he cares for Carreen. He interrupts himself to ask Mrs. Tarleton to take Scarlett and Grandma Fontaine into the house, out of the hot sun. Grandma Fontaine knows exactly why Will does this and warns Scarlett many people will resent her for allowing Suellen to marry a Cracker, even though it is an excellent decision. Scarlett basks in her approval until Grandma Fontaine offers that Ashley is helpless and Melly reminds her of Ellen. Scarlett bristles, then accepts (although it is not totally true) that Grandma Fontaine is just trying to keep her mind off Gerald's burial.

Remembering the promise made to Pork the night he was shot robbing a hen house to feed them, Scarlett gives an astonished Pork Gerald's gold watch. Ashley is next in her office. He blames himself for Scarlett's marriage to Frank, saying he should not have let her go to Atlanta for the tax money; somehow, he should have gotten it himself. She begs him to come to Atlanta to "help" her. He refuses several times, not wanting to continue living off her largess. She offers him a half-interest in the mill. He insists the offer is still charity because the half-interest is a gift; therefore, he cannot accept.

Scarlett keeps urging him to accept the offer until he finally admits he can no longer keep himself to the promise made in the

orchard not to act on his desire for her. Scarlett begins to cry, causing Melanie to come investigate the reason for her sobs. In retell-
ing the conversation, Scarlett counts on Melly's goodness which
will make her persuade her husband to take the offer. The two
women bully Ashley into agreeing. Melly thinks it is all a ploy of
Scarlett's to bring her back to the Atlanta she misses so much.

Carreen goes to the convent; Will and Suellen marry; and
Ashley, Melanie, and Beau go to Atlanta bringing Dilcey with them.
Melanie chooses the house behind Pittypat's because the yards are
joined. India, Ashley's sister, joins the Wilkes since Honey, their
other sister with whom she'd been living, married.

Ashley buys the least expensive furniture in Frank's store on
credit, refusing his and Scarlett's offered gifts of expensive furniture. Melanie, although not well, runs a happy home (usually full
of company), becomes the informal leader of the Old Guard of
Southern women, heads the Saturday Night Musical Circle, is sec-
retary for both the Association for the Beautification of Graves of
Our Glorious Dead and the Sewing Circle for Widows and Orphans
of the Confederacy, is on the board of lady managers of the Orphans' Home, collects books for the Young Men's Library Association, and is a member of the Thespians.

Scarlett and Frank visit their home often, Scarlett with hopes
of seeing Ashley. While all the visitors tell stories of the war, she
wants only to forget it. During her confinement, both mills lose
money. She resolves to hire Johnnie Gallegher, who works for
Tommy Wellburn, to manage Hugh's mill and lease convicts for
labor instead of hiring unreliable, drunken freed slaves. Frank is
vehemently opposed to this idea. While Scarlett finds Hugh incom-
petent, she excuses the same errors in Ashley's management of the
second mill. She decides her business suffers too much when she
has a baby and so won't have any more.

She gives birth to a daughter, Ella Lorena, in the midst of Klan
activity and Yankee arrests which create fear throughout the town.
Three weeks later, she wants to see her mills and intends to drive
herself, but Frank forbids it so Scarlett runs over to Melly in a temper. Melanie sends Archie, one of the homeless she lets sleep in
her cellar, to drive for Scarlett and protect her. Frank agrees to this.
Archie announces he hates "niggers," Yankees, talkative women.

Soon, other ladies ask Scarlett for Archie's services as a bodyguard.

Frank and Ashley begin to stay out nights, saying they are at meetings or with sick friends, while the rest of their families gather at Melly's under Archie's protection. When Scarlett mentions leasing convicts in front of Archie, he says he won't stay if she does and tells her he was a convict for 40 years, having murdered his wife for having an affair with his brother. He was pardoned for fighting Yankees in Milledgeville where he lost his leg and eye. He tells Scarlett Melly knew all this about him before the first night he stayed in her cellar.

The legislature refuses to ratify an amendment giving the freed slaves the vote. Ashley warns the Yankees will retaliate. At this point, Uncle Henry directs Archie to drive Scarlett home, away from the crowd in front of a saloon where she asked Archie to stop. Scarlett proceeds to lease the convicts. True to his word, Archie refuses to drive for her anymore. There is disapproval all round for this leasing and of Scarlett for doing it.

Scarlett gives Johnnie a free hand in dealing with the convicts and he tells her to stay away from the mill so as not to interfere, which affords her more time to sell. Initially, Ashley refuses to work with them, but once cajoled into agreement, does a poor job of overseeing the convicts.

Analysis

When Grandma Fontaine tells Scarlett she's good with business but not with people, she's succinctly naming a great lack in Scarlett. Perhaps it is Scarlett's egocentricity which keeps her from understanding, or even wanting to make an attempt to understand, other people. She is not dumbfounded, but only impatient, when Ashley says he has to earn his own living and she dismisses this need for independence as too trivial for discussion. Later, when he is manager of her mill in Atlanta as she coerced him into being, she doesn't connect the dead look in his eyes with this lack of doing for himself.

Apparently Grandma Fontaine is not the only one who thinks of him as helpless. Ashley seems to be in great pain as he struggles against Scarlett's coddling and smothering. He knows he needs to resist her efforts to keep making his life as easy as possible (under the circumstances) but gives up when Melanie joins forces with Scarlett. In Atlanta, he makes a token gesture of self-assertion by insisting upon paying for his own furniture on credit, rather than accepting yet more life-easing gifts from Scarlett.

Will, as the clear thinker, tries to tell Scarlett to let Ashley go but she refuses to hear. She knows nothing of Carreen's vocation and her deep grief, having spent no thought on her little sister. While Will cares deeply for Carreen, he sees she needs to be a nun. Scarlett is unaware of the depth of Suellen's need for money, a husband, and a family. Will sees it and acts upon it to his advantage, as a way of staying on at Tara after all the proper chaperons have left. Will even sees that Suellen never loved Frank; she just needed to be married.

Scarlett's inward focus limits her, as does other people attributing thoughtful motives to her selfishness. Even Melanie thinks Scarlett's inveigling Ashley into managing the mill is a tactic to return her to the Atlanta where she grew up. Scarlett does not plant this thought in Melly's mind, but being so good herself, Melly can only think of goodness in others. This is frustrating to Scarlett, however (as Grandma Fontaine says) not being good with people, she cannot explain herself or her feelings to Melly. While Rhett understands her, Will seems more to simply accept what she's doing rather than understand her or question her motives.

Study Questions

1. How did Suellen cause her father's death?

2. Why does Will want to marry Suellen?

3. Why is Carreen going to enter a convent?

4. Why does Ashley want to go to New York?

5. Why does Melly prevent him from doing so?

6. Once in Atlanta, what does Melly do?

7. What happens to the freedman accused of rape?

8. Why does Melly send Archie to Scarlett?

9. Why does Archie resign?

10. What does Scarlett do when she returns to the mills after her daughter's birth?

Answers

1. Drunk from the brandy Suellen gave him to muddle his thinking, Gerald attempts to jump a fence with a horse. But this is not his usual horse and it refuses to jump, causing Gerald to go sailing over its head and land in such a way as to break his neck.

2. In order to live at the Tara he loves and works so hard for, Will has to marry Suellen.

3. When Brent Tarleton was killed in the war, Carreen's heart broke. Although she cares for Will and speaks freely to him, she is not in love with anyone except Brent and feels a religious life is the only one she wants now.

4. A friend with whom Ashley took the Grand Tour of Europe before the war has offered him a job in his father's New York bank.

5. Scarlett insists to Melly that she needs Ashley to manage the mill since she cannot get anyone else and she herself is pregnant.

6. Melanie buys the small house behind Pittypat's, for the yards are adjoining. Ashley's spinster, forbidding sister, India, comes to live with them.

7. The Klan raids the jail and hangs him to spare the victim the shame of testifying in court.

8. Three weeks after Ella Lorna's birth, Scarlett is eager to return to her mills, but Frank forbids her to drive alone in this atmosphere. Melly gives shelter, in her cellar, to homeless people. One of them, Archie, is a fearsome ex-convict with one eye and one leg. Melanie asks Archie to be Scarlett's bodyguard and drive her, with Frank's approval.

9. When Scarlett talks of leasing convicts for labor (since the freed slaves either come to work at the mills drunk, late, or

not at all), Archie tells her that if she does, he will no longer be her bodyguard. He says it's "murder" on the convicts since no one watches out for their welfare when they're leased.

10. Scarlett demotes Hugh Elsing to driving the lumber wagon, hires Johnnie Gallegher—although he is known to be a hard overseer—and leases the convicts.

Chapters 43-45

Summary

Rhett returns after an absence of several months. He chides Scarlett for leasing convicts and hiring Johnnie Gallegher to manage them and the mill. She asks why he goes to New Orleans so often. He responds that his legal ward, a schoolboy, is there and asks her to keep this information to herself. He also went to Charleston because his father died.

His father had disowned him as a youth, making it necessary for his mother to lie in order to see him in secret. Rhett's mother and sister were destitute since the war because his father refused to accept Rhett's "tainted" money. They lived on the charity of their friends and whatever small amounts his brother (who also refused Rhett's money) could send to them. One of these friends is Scarlett's Aunt Eulalie, who shares whatever Scarlett sends with them. Once his father dies, Rhett buys his mother and sister a house and hires servants for them, allowing the neighbors to think the money comes from his father's nonexistent life insurance policy.

Rhett is distressed, even though her loan from him is repaid, that Scarlett broke her promise that the money would not go towards Ashley's support. He explains Ashley would be better off dead because the world he knows died in the war and he no longer knows what to do with himself. Rhett will no longer lend her money, should she need it, because she broke her promise by hiring Ashley to manage the mill which Rhett's money helped her buy. After calling her a rouge for legally cheating the poor by buying their mortgages, he leaves with a warning that Frank should stay home at night more often.

As Ashley predicted, conditions in Atlanta become worse af-

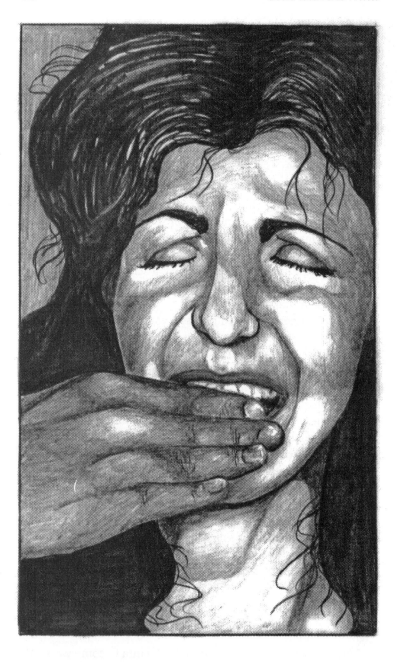

ter the legislature refuses to ratify the amendment giving the freedmen the vote. Georgia is now under martial law, having been declared in rebellion. There is no safety anywhere, but Scarlett
continues to drive herself to the mills with only a pistol for protection. As she passes through Shantytown (a ragtag conglomeration
of criminals, poor whites, and prostitutes) she is stopped by Big
Sam, the former foreman of Tara, who is hiding in Shantytown now
while trying to get back to Tara.

He had been captured by a Northern colonel and taken north
but was confused by the courtesy and equality he was shown and
the underlying feeling he had there of being disliked and distrusted.
She offers him the job of carriage man for her, but he just wants to
go home. She persists until he admits he is hiding there because
he killed a white man. Scarlett says she will send him to Tara that
very night and arranges to meet him at dusk.

Scarlett goes to the mill, where she finally realizes that Johnnie
is whipping and starving the leased convicts. She thinks Johnnie is
selling the food she sends him for them. He threatens to resign
when she demands payment for the food and says she will have it
delivered daily rather than monthly, henceforth. Scarlett agrees to
take the money from his wages and let the matter stand since she
needs him right now. She knows this is the end of the matter and
Johnnie is the victor. It troubles her that she might eventually be
the cause of these men's deaths if she continues to allow him to
beat and starve them, but she rationalizes her feeling.

That evening, while waiting near Shantytown to meet Big Sam,
a black man and a white man attempt to rob her. The black man
rips open her dress, thinking she's hidden money in her bosom,
while the white man stops the horse. Big Sam appears and screams
at her to go. As she does, she runs over the white man. Big Sam
catches up, telling her he thinks he killed the black man.

Frank takes charge of getting Big Sam home once Big Sam assures him Scarlett is scared, not hurt. His calm and authoritative
manner inflames Scarlett. That night, he goes out again saying it's
a political meeting. At Melly's, Scarlett keeps attempting to discuss
the experience but Melly keeps changing the subject. Melly and
India are very nervous and pass meaningful looks at each other.
Archie is sullen and silent. India tells Scarlett this afternoon's ex-

perience is just what she deserves and now she's put their men's lives in danger.

Rhett arrives demanding to know where Frank and Ashley are just as Melly hushes India. He knows there's a trap planned by the Yankees. Melly tells him they're at the old half-burned Sullivan plantation on Decatur Road near Shantytown. Rhett rushes out, telling them to say nothing when the Yankees come. Melly confesses to Scarlett that Frank and Ashley are in the Klan as are all the other men they know. Archie adds they will annihilate the Shantytown settlement if they can and it is her fault if they're all killed.

A Yankee officer arrives asking to see Frank and Ashley. When Melly tells him they are at a meeting at Frank's store, he says this is not so and he will wait outside until they return. The soldiers surround the house as Archie commands the women to sew. Melly hears a sound. It is Rhett singing "Marching Through Georgia." Two other drunken voices join in. The captain attempts to arrest Hugh Elsing and Ashley, but Melly plays the outraged wife, making a show of throwing Rhett out for having gotten her husband drunk again.

When the officer tries again to arrest them, Rhett swears they were all at Belle Watling's for a drunken party. Melly pretends to faint at this shocking news. The officer agrees to postpone Ashley's arrest until the following morning when Rhett offers 50 witnesses in their defense, but still takes Hugh with him. Ashley has a severe shoulder wound and passes out. India is sent for old Dr. Dean since Dr. Meade is involved in the night's activities.

Despite his protests at taking orders from Rhett, Melly tells Archie to do what Rhett says—go to the old Sullivan plantation and burn the robes the Klan members pushed up into the largest chimney, then take the two bodies there to the lot behind Belle's house and place fired pistols in their hands. Rhett explains to Melly that Belle already has a list of the men she is to swear were at her "sporting house" this night. In order to substantiate the claims of having been there, the men staged a fight and allowed themselves to be dragged out by Belles' bouncers. Dr. Meade, Uncle Henry, and old man Merriwether were among the men there. Old Dr. Dean arrives to tend to Ashley. Rhett draws Scarlett out of the room to tell her Frank is dead, shot through the head.

Analysis

Scarlett remains focused on herself while the world around her changes quickly and dramatically. Because she refuses to listen to warnings about making it more dangerous for the men by driving through Shantytown alone, Big Sam has killed another man. Because she doesn't want to think about the Klan, she doesn't question where her husband and Ashley go so often at night. Rhett warns her specifically that she could cause someone's death if she persists in disregarding the sanctions not to expose herself to danger.

Everyone but she knows the Klan is active to retaliate for crimes against white women. Everyone but she knows her husband, Ashley, and all the other men in town are members. Everyone but she tries to avoid causing incidences in which the Klan will eventually be involved, leading to further danger for the town's men.

By selfishly pursuing her business without taking these precautions, she indirectly causes the death of her own husband, the potential arrest of Ashley (not to mention his wound), and the arrest of Hugh Elsing.

While she is not being vindictive, she is so thoughtless of all but her own interests that she is thoroughly jarred by all this news. While her family benefits from the financial gain she wants for herself, she is becoming a dangerous person. While she hates the Klan, it is working to protect her. There's a certain amount of immaturity here since she blithely goes about her business, taking little account of the world around her. While the townspeople work together to survive, she is childlike in that her vision extends only to her immediate gratification without thought of its effect on others.

Study Questions

1. Why has Rhett been gone for so many months?
2. Why will he no longer be available to Scarlett for loans?
3. Why is Big Sam sent to Tara?
4. What does Scarlett discover about Johnnie Gallegher?
5. How does she endanger the town's men?

6. Of what are Frank and Ashley members?

7. What is it that Melly and India know?

8. Why does Rhett arrive at Melly's unannounced that night?

9. How does he prevent Ashley's arrest?

10. Why does Rhett speak to Scarlett alone?

Answers

1. Rhett has a legal ward, a boy, who goes to school in New Orleans. He goes there often to visit him. But this time, Rhett also went to Charleston where his family lives.

2. Scarlett made a bargain with Rhett when she borrowed the money to buy the mill that none of this money would go towards Ashley's support. By coercing Ashley to take the manager's position at the mill, she's broken this agreement and Rhett will loan her nothing more.

3. Big Sam worked for the Confederate Army until his captain was killed. He tried to hide then because there was no one to tell him what to do and he had heard Tara was burned down. A Yankee colonel took him to Savannah and then north with him. He stayed until he got homesick. On his way back to Tara, he heard a Yankee soldier say something he couldn't tolerate and choked him to death. He's been hiding in Shantytown for two days, but fears for his life since the soldier he killed was white. He needs to escape.

4. Johnnie Gallegher is whipping and starving the leased convicts. He is selling the food which Scarlett sends for them once a month.

5. Scarlett continues to drive through Shantytown with only a pistol for protection. Rhett has warned her that if she is accosted, as is likely, during this drive, the men of the town will feel it necessary to defend her honor by retaliating via the Ku Klux Klan. That, in turn, will cause the Yankees to become even more stringent in their punishment of the townsmen.

6. Frank and Ashley are members of the Ku Klux Klan, which has arisen to retaliate against attacks on white women from drunken or overly aggressive freedmen.

7. Melly and India know Ashley and Frank are going with the Klan to avenge Scarlett's being mauled by a black robber that evening.

8. Rhett was playing poker with two drunken Yankee soldiers who told him the Klan is walking into a trap that night. He wants to know where they are so he can warn them.

9. Rhett goes to the cellar of the half-burned Sullivan plantation on Decatur Road near Shantytown to warn them. Two men are dead and Ashley wounded, but he manages to wrap Ashley in his cloak and convince the Yankee, Captain Jaffery (who has awaited Ashley's return to arrest him), that Ashley is drunk and spent the night carousing and womanizing at Belle Watling's. Rhett has arranged for 50 witnesses to swear the Klan members were at Belle's.

10. While old Dr. Dean, with Melanie and India assisting, tends to Ashley, Rhett draws Scarlett out of the room. She thinks he's going to tell her Frank was at Belle's also. Instead, he tells her Frank is dead from a shot through the head.

Chapters 46-47

Summary

When Captain Jaffery gets no answers, he arrests some men and orders Belle and her girls to appear for questioning in the morning. Meanwhile, Frank and Tommy Wellburn's bodies are placed behind Belle's place to make it look as if they killed each other in a drunken fight over one of Belle's girls. The whole town resents having to rely on Belle and Rhett for their alibis. While the Yankees are amused by the alibis, they feel kindly toward Scarlett in her loss. Mrs. Meade thinks the alibi is Rhett's enormous, but lifesaving, joke on the people that disdain him.

Belle calls at Melly's house, but stays in the closed carriage to warn her the note of gratitude Melanie sent is unnecessary and dangerous if the Yankees get it. She insists it is unseemly for Melly to call on her as she intends.

Scarlett regrets causing Frank's death but only because she fears God will punish her for making Frank so unhappy. As she rests in bed, ruminating and drinking brandy, Rhett arrives saying he needs to see her about some business Frank and he had in common. That turns out to be a lie designed to make Pittypat leave the two of them alone together. Once alone, he derides Scarlett's secret drinking.

As he comforts her, she unburdens herself, telling him she's afraid to die and go to hell for marrying Frank when he loved Suellen. She tells him of her reoccurring nightmare of being back at Tara right after Ellen's death and being so hungry, then running away from something only to wake up before she's safe.

Rhett talks her into seeing that she is an opportunist, announces he is going to England the next day, and asks her to marry him. He has a difficult time convincing her he's serious. She says she won't marry again, doesn't love him, wants to go home to Tara, and doesn't like being married. Rhett reads her hunger for Ashley in her face. He kisses her into accepting his proposal which surprises her.

Upon his questioning, she acknowledges she does not love him but is fond of him and is marrying him partly for his money and partly because she can be truthful with him and not have to play the silly fool or tell lies as she must with other men. She asks him to bring a diamond ring from England. The ring he returns with is vulgar in its size. When they announce their engagement, the entire town ostracizes both of them, never having approved of either of them individually. Scalawags and Carpetbaggers are hated in Atlanta and, now, are Rhett's only friends.

Mammy is the only other person whose opinion Scarlett values. Mammy thinks Ellen would heartily disapprove of Scarlett's marrying "trash" as she calls Rhett. She refuses to leave when Scarlett attempts to send her back to Tara, but she sees clearly who and what Scarlett and Rhett are. On their honeymoon, Rhett confesses he'd love to have Mammy's respect but Scarlett cannot think why.

Analysis

While Rhett is certain about who he is and what effect he has on other people, he finds himself frustrated with Scarlett's limited feelings. She knows him well enough for him to tell her about his ward and the bad blood with his father, but not well enough to see he is deeply in love with her. She considers him someone of whom she's fond, but allows her desire for Ashley to blind her to Rhett's love, even though she knows Rhett is as frank as she is. For once, Rhett is not enjoying her frankness when she admits his money is part of her reason for marrying him.

Rhett is hurt. That is obvious from the diamond ring he brings her from England. It is so large as to be a caricature of the real thing. Due to her egocentricity and delight at being able to make her neighbors envious, she doesn't see this. Nor does Scarlett see Rhett willfully rein in his feelings when she calmly proclaims she doesn't love him. This marriage may have been thought about years before when he first saw her at Twelve Oaks or later in Atlanta when he asked her to be his mistress, but what Scarlett is missing is that, despite his own disavowal of love for her, he is in love with her.

Study Questions

1. What does Captain Jaffery tell Belle Watling and her girls to do?

2. Where are Frank and Tommy's bodies?

3. What do the townspeople resent?

4. Why does Belle come to Melly's house?

5. Why does Scarlett regret being the cause of Frank's death?

6. What has she taken to doing secretly?

7. To what does Rhett tell Pittypat he and Scarlett must tend?

8. What is Scarlett's nightmare?

9. What does Rhett ask Scarlett?

10. What does she ask Rhett to bring her?

Answers

1. Captain Jaffery tells Belle Watling she and her girls will have to appear before the provost marshall. They do and she gives her word that all 12 men under suspicion were at her house the night in question and are actually regular customers who always come on Wednesday night.

2. Under Rhett's orders, Archie moves Frank and Tommy's bodies from the old Sullivan plantation to the lot behind Belle's place.

3. While Rhett saves all the men who are under suspicion of Klan activity with his lies, the town resents the laughter he has caused among the Yankees which is directed at them.

4. True to form, Melly sends Belle a note of gratitude. Belle comes to her house in a closed carriage to tell Melly that her note was unnecessary since she remembers how kind Melanie was to her during the war when she wanted to donate money to the hospital.

5. Scarlett regrets having been the cause of Frank's death because she is afraid of dying and going to hell. That's where she thinks she will be punished for marrying Frank and making him unhappy by shaming and bullying him.

6. Scarlett has been secretly drinking brandy since her pregnancy with Ella. Now her drinking is getting out of hand and she knows, despite gargling with cologne afterwards, Mammy suspects.

7. Rhett pretends he had business with Frank that Scarlett must help him settle immediately since he will be leaving for England in the morning. This is not true. He says this simply so Pittypat will allow him to see Scarlett, who is resting, and talk alone with her.

8. Scarlett's nightmare takes place back at Tara right after Ellen dies. Everyone is hungry and expecting her to feed them. She is hungry, too. Then she is running in a mist to avoid being caught, but wakes up before she is safe.

9. Rhett asks Scarlett if she will marry him. He realizes she will

never be his mistress. He loves her, which he cannot admit because she tells him she's only fond of him.

10. Scarlett asks Rhett to bring her a diamond ring from England. She especially wants a big one.

Suggested Essay Topics

1. The Ku Klux Klan plays a prominent role in this section of the book. From your reading, detail its origin, members, activities, and the outcome of these activities.

2. It has been said that children are the silent victims of war. Using Wade as your example, either prove or disprove this statement. Be specific.

3. What part did the Scalawags and Carpetbaggers play in the downfall of the plantation system and how did this personally impact on Scarlett and the Tara family?

4. Honor has been the guiding principle in Ashley's life. How has his conception of this both determined the course of his actions and prevented him from doing what would be easy or convenient?

SECTION SIX

Gone with the Wind, Part V

Chapters 48-50

Summary

As we move into Part V of the book, Scarlett and Rhett are on their honeymoon in New Orleans. Scarlett thoroughly enjoys Rhett's Carpetbagger, Scalawag, and speculator friends, preferring to ignore his past activities. He buys her stylish clothes and she buys gifts for the family. Rhett reminds her to get Mammy a present, but she refuses saying Mammy was hateful, so he buys Mammy one. What Scarlett enjoys the most in New Orleans is the food and liquor.

While discussing how he invests his money, Rhett tells her he is going to have a house built near Pittypat's and they will stay in the bridal suite of the National Hotel until it is completed. She chooses a garish style even as he warns her not to expect the Old Guard to come to their home even if they, the Butlers, are rich. He urges her to continue with the store and the mills reminding her, once again, he will not contribute to Ashley's support.

The Ladies' Sewing Circle for the Widows and Orphans of the Confederacy meet in Melanie's home. They heatedly discuss whether or not to call on Scarlett, but Melly overhears. She tells them that if they will not call on Scarlett, they should no longer call on her. India slips out while the others cry, concede to Melanie,

and embrace her. Later, Uncle Henry concurs with the ladies' opinion of Scarlett as unworthy.

The families of the men involved in the Klan incident do call, but with less and less frequency and do not invite the Butlers to their homes. Scarlett is so busy with her "new" friends that she barely notices. The rest of her spare time is spent overseeing the building of their new home. Rhett tells her, once it is finished, that it is not as attractive as she thinks, nor is she as socially astute as she thinks. She intends to change the name of Frank's store to the catchy "Caveat Emptorium" but discards the idea once Ashley interprets the new name for her.

As the result of a serious argument about money not changing a person, Scarlett begins to sulk so Rhett leaves for New Orleans for four days, taking Wade with him. Scarlett swallows her anger when he returns, putting all her energy into planning their first "crush." Scarlett invites everyone she knows, whether she likes them or not. Of the Old Guard, only Melanie and Ashley, Pittypat, Uncle Henry, Dr. and Mrs. Meade, and Grandpa Merriwether attend. The rest decline the invitation when they learn, two days before the party, that Rhett's friend, the Republican Governor Bullock, is invited and will attend. As soon as he arrives, the small group of the Old Guard who do come leave rather than have to meet him.

From that night forth, Scarlett is no longer a member of the Old Guard; they have cast her out. At first, she is hurt, then she becomes genuinely indifferent. She receives all manner of new people except for those in the Yankee army. She has contempt for her new friends but enjoys them at the same time. She no longer bothers about Rhett. While Rhett listens to her plans and schemes, he seems to see through them which infuriates Scarlett.

Scarlett becomes pregnant and threatens to abort the child. Rhett is terribly upset, explaining this could kill her; he demands she carry the baby full term. When the baby is born, Melly is afraid that Rhett may be disappointed it's not a boy but Mammy tells her he is delighted (which changes Mammy's opinion of him favorably).

Wade is terrified when his mother goes into labor. He is told she is ill and packed off to Pittypat's with his baby sister, Ella. There is no one there to pay attention to him, so he takes the opportunity to slip home again since he thinks his mother may die. Mammy discovers him there and scoldingly sends him back to Pittypat's but he doesn't go. He is discovered again, this time by Melanie who tells him Dr. Meade brought a baby and to go back to Pittypat's. He remains, still convinced his mother is dying, until Rhett discovers him hiding in the dining room and spends time talking to him and reassuring him. They share a toast as Rhett wards off Wade's ques-

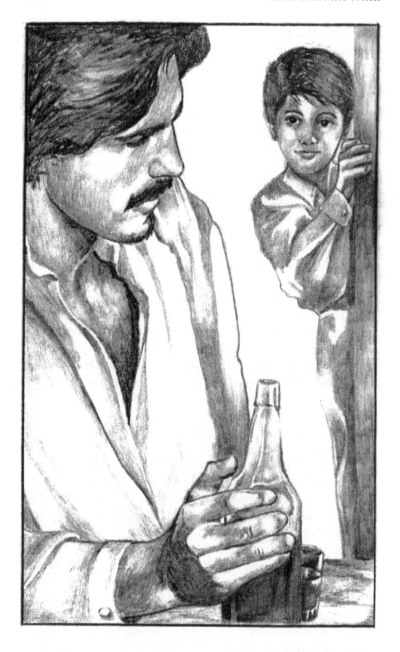

tions about Rhett's having any other little boys.

Mammy enters, calling Rhett "Mist' Rhett" and wearing the petticoat she had made of the red silk Rhett brought her from his honeymoon in New Orleans which Scarlett said Mammy would refuse. There is a truce between them, with Mammy already respecting Rhett who is totally besotted with his daughter. Rhett continues to dote on Eugenie Victoria as Scarlett continues to feel it unseemly for a father to be so involved with his child.

Analysis

Scarlett seems to be beyond all hope at this point. Her limited vision has cost her even the courtesy of any member of the Old Guard and her contempt for her new, ill-bred, classless friends will eventually estrange them. She no longer bothers about her husband, almost convinces herself she couldn't care less if Melanie calls, and alienates Mammy. She never seems to have time for her son and barely thinks of Ella.

Her reason for wanting an abortion is so she will not lose her waistline. Apparently, all her thoughts are just as shallow. Her house, its decoration, her clothes, the food and drink, all are designed to flaunt her affluence despite the poverty of the genteel folk. The false society she surrounds herself with is also shallow and ostentatious. There must be some part of her that knows each of these people is only using her as an entry into Southern society; why else the contempt for the very people she calls "friends" and entertains?

Will is far away but Rhett is right there seeing through her illusions and grand gestures. He is forever warning her to watch herself, to think of her future, to realize who she is. She becomes more and more angry with him, but loving her, he does not stop the warnings. He sees himself clearly and can accept who he is. He wants her to see herself, whether or not she can accept who she is.

The fact that she still has the nightmare, despite having more money than she'd ever considered and a surfeit of the finest food whenever she chooses, seems to prove that she is still tortured. She goes to Rhett for solace after a nightmare, but cannot see it when he tries to point out what a nightmare she's making of her life. She thinks she is enjoying drinking so much and so often, but is embarrassed by the next day's hangover. Trapped deep within Scarlett, there are still vestiges of the ladylike behavior Ellen and Mammy instilled in her as a child.

Study Questions

1. What do Rhett and Scarlett do on their honeymoon?

2. Back in Atlanta again, where do Rhett and Scarlett stay?

3. What does The Ladies' Sewing Circle for the Widows and Orphans of the Confederacy discuss?

4. About what does Rhett try to warn Scarlett?

5. Why isn't Scarlett's "crush" a success?

6. Why is Scarlett cast out by the Old Guard?

7. How does Melanie fear she's offended Scarlett?

8. Why does Scarlett want an abortion?

9. Why is Wade afraid during the birth of the new baby?

10. When does Mammy begin to develop respect for Rhett?

Answers

1. Rhett and Scarlett have fun on their honeymoon in New Orleans.

2. Rhett and Scarlett stay in the bridal suite of the National Hotel when they return from their honeymoon in New Orleans. Rhett has decided to have a large house built for them near Pittypat's.

3. The Ladies' Sewing Circle for the Widows and Orphans of the Confederacy discusses whether or not to call on Scarlett.

4. Rhett tries to warn Scarlett about her present actions undermining her future.

5. Scarlett's "crush," or combination reception-ball, is not a success because she invites Governor Bullock. Her Old Guard friends hear a rumor to this effect two days before the party and decline her invitations.

6. Once Scarlett invites Bullock to her crush, the Old Guard (except for the select few named in the answer above) refuse to have any dealings with her.

7. When Scarlett explodes at Melly for leaving the party early the night before, Melly tells her she had not believed the rumor that Bullock would be there and so attended. Scarlett angrily proclaims it an insult for Melly to have even considered not coming.

8. Scarlett wants an abortion when she discovers she is pregnant with Rhett's child.

9. After being packed off to Pittypat's along with his baby sister, seven-year-old Wade is terrified his mother will die because he is told she is sick.

10. Mammy begins to develop respect for Rhett when she sees his delight at the birth of his daughter.

Chapters 51-53

Summary

Contemplating her slightly larger waistline, Scarlett decides not to have any more children. She goes to the mill where she and Ashley examine the books and is disappointed at how poorly he's done in comparison to Johnnie Gallegher. Ashley explains he cannot be as harsh on the convicts as Johnnie is and blames Rhett for poisoning her when she tells Ashley he must be harsh. Her belief that Ashley loves her is intensified as he criticizes Rhett.

She tells Rhett she wants separate bedrooms to ensure no future pregnancies, but doesn't tell him it's also to be true to Ashley. Rhett tells Scarlett he could divorce her for this but won't; he's tired of her sexually. She cannot think how to tell Ashley she and Rhett have separate bedrooms, so doesn't.

Wade tells Scarlett and Rhett that everyone but he is invited to Raoul Ricard's (Maybelle and Rene's son) birthday party. Scarlett pays no attention but Rhett questions him, discovering he is never invited to the Old Guard's grandchildren's parties and doesn't en-

joy the parties he goes to given by Scarlett's new friends for their children. Rhett answers his questions about being in the army and being wounded in a positive light, even though it entails some lying, so Wade will be proud of him.

Rhett swears to himself that Bonnie Blue (his pet name for his daughter) will not be ashamed of him nor will doors be closed to her as she grows up, because of her parents' behavior prior to her birth. Scarlett thinks their money will solve all of these problems. Rhett knows they need help to ensure a place for Bonnie in society and vows to cultivate the ladies of the Old Guard for his daughter's sake. He insists Scarlett be his help mate in this bid for respectability. Despite the difficulties in the political situation, Rhett begins to change his behavior using his charm and generosity to slowly inveigle his way back into society.

Except for the time he spends in his bank where he "works," Rhett is with Bonnie continuously. Although the Old Guard is still suspicious of anyone who associated with Bullock, over time Rhett slowly begins to be accepted. Due to her fear of the dark, Bonnie sleeps in Rhett's room with a lamp on all night even though Scarlett thinks a spanking would be more appropriate and that this is retribution for her request for separate bedrooms.

The lamp goes out one night when Rhett is not home. He arrives to hear Bonnie screaming, quiets her and puts her to bed, then blames Scarlett who says she doesn't want Bonnie to grow up "nervous and cowardly." Rhett is incensed at what he considers her inhumanity and reminds her it was very recently that he comforted her when she had nightmares, too. It is Bonnie's dislike of the smell of liquor on his breath which causes Rhett to modify his drinking.

Melanie gives Ashley a surprise party for his birthday, his first party since the barbecue at Twelve Oaks before the war. Archie offers to hang the garden lanterns while Ashley is inside eating dinner. Scarlett and India are helping Melly prepare when Scarlett mentions she has to go to the lumberyard to pay the drivers and Hugh. Ashley is going there in the late afternoon so Melly asks Scarlett to keep him there until five o'clock to ensure the surprise is not spoiled. Scarlett realizes that she is perturbed Melly has not asked her to receive the guests along with India and Pittypat.

She arrives at the lumberyard later than she expected. As she greets Ashley, he asks her why she isn't home preparing for his party, explaining all the men invited told him so he wouldn't make other plans that night. As they banter, Scarlett is surprised that Ashley's touch on her hand doesn't excite her. He admits he is not a great man and has had to rely on Scarlett, but she denies this. He points out that he and Rhett are alike in background and beliefs about the war, but she stops him again. He reminds her of the past but she feels this is dangerous for her. Scarlett soon shunts aside this feeling and joins him in the memories. She begins to cry and he comforts her, in friendship. Just then, India, Archie, and Mrs. Elsing enter to find Scarlett in Ashley's arms. Scarlett fears what will happen once they tell Melanie as she is sure they will. She knows no one will come to her defense.

She goes home to hide in her room, planning to say she is ill and cannot attend Ashley's party. Rhett comes to her room and castigates her for trying to avoid the people he's so carefully cultivated. Archie did tell Rhett what he had seen, but Rhett refuses to hear Scarlett's explanations. He taunts her by calling her a coward, practically dresses her himself, and drives her into Melly's house. As she prepares herself to be snubbed by all, Melly comes through the crowd complementing Scarlett on her dress and asking her to help receive since India could not come.

Analysis

Scarlett's chickens are coming home to roost, but she cannot see it yet. Rhett is aghast that seven-year-old Wade is paying for his mother's past conduct but Scarlett doesn't know what he's talking about. Rhett fears for Bonnie's future but, again, Scarlett is puzzled. There seems to be no connection in her mind between the way she and Rhett have behaved and the way her children are being treated by the Old Guard. On some level, she sees things simplistically because it is so convenient for her. A children's party is nothing to get upset about, in her way of thinking. Rhett sees it as symbolic of the life the children can expect to have and, as the realist, intends to change that.

When Rhett speaks plainly to her, she understands only what he tells her to do, not why. He makes it clear she is, at least, not to hinder his attempts to brighten their children's futures. She not only doesn't understand the reasons behind his instructions, but also does not expend the energy to interpret the signals her emotions give her. When Ashley takes her hands at the mill, she doesn't feel the "spark" she expects. She spends a moment acknowledging this to herself, then dismisses it until he comforts her in her sadness and only then does she realize the value of his friendship.

All her life, she has defied the conventions of society to gain her selfish desires. It seems almost to be a thoughtless habit now. While she may have felt some slight remorse once or twice in the past, especially when Frank died, this was selfish, too. She cares only for what happens to her, how she feels, what she wants now. Rhett no sooner tells her not to undermine his attempts to secure a place in society for the children than she allows herself to be caught in Ashley's embrace (even though she now loves him as a friend with whom she's shared her past).

A new wrinkle here is that she seems genuinely concerned about Melly. She thinks it is because she fears Melly will leave Ashley and that would shame him, but there is that split second when she just plainly fears losing Melanie's love without understanding why.

Study Questions

1. Why does Scarlett tell Rhett she wants separate bedrooms?
2. Why is Wade unhappy?
3. What does Rhett decide about the children?
4. With whom does he spend almost all of his time?
5. Why does Bonnie begin screaming?
6. What is Melanie giving Ashley?
7. Why does Scarlett go to the lumber yard?
8. What are Ashley and Scarlett discovered doing?
9. What does Scarlett try to do after they are discovered?
10. Why won't Rhett let her do this?

Answers

1. Initially, Scarlett blames her expanding waistline on preg-

nancies. Since Rhett won't allow abortions, abstinence is the only birth control she knows and she thinks the separate bedrooms will cool Rhett's ardor.

2. Wade is bored on a rainy day. He cannot visit or have someone come to play because all the other children are at Raoul's birthday party. Rhett immediately realizes the Old Guard has ostracized Wade for his mother and stepfather's past behavior.

3. Rhett decides he cannot allow the children to be shunned this way. If this is how Wade is treated, he knows if he doesn't make some changes, it will be the same for Bonnie. He begins to curry the favor of the Old Guard matriarchs.

4. Rhett is always with Bonnie when he is not working. He takes her for rides and walks, stopping often to say hello to the townspeople and make small talk. He lets Bonnie do the talking, knowing she will charm them.

5. When Bonnie is two, she develops a fear of the dark.

6. Melly is giving Ashley a surprise birthday party.

7. Scarlett is going to the lumberyard to pay the drivers and Hugh.

8. When Scarlett and Ashley are alone in the office of the lumber mill, Scarlett becomes sad and begins to cry. Ashley silently takes her in his arms, as a friend, and this stops the flow of tears. It is at this moment that Archie and India arrive with Mrs. Elsing right behind them.

9. Scarlett tries to hide in her bedroom. She knows the story will be embellished by the time of tonight's party and doesn't want to face the lies.

10. Rhett won't let Scarlett hide in her room because he cannot allow her to be known as a coward on top of her reputation as a trollop. His most important reason for this is that by staying home, she would further ruin Bonnie's chances for a secure future in society.

Chapters 54-56

Summary

Once safely home from Ashley's party, Scarlett is an emotional wreck. After silently thinking in her room, she goes to get a drink when a very drunken Rhett asks her to join him in the dining room. She thinks it best not to let him see she fears him. He gives her a drink, telling her he knows all about her secret drinking, and forces her to sit down to discuss the evening with him.

He divulges that he knows Melly doesn't believe Ashley and Scarlett are lovers; she's too honorable " . . . to conceive of dishonor in anyone she loves" and she loves both Ashley and Scarlett. He reveals he knows she has been lusting for Ashley since before they met, even as he was making love to her. She leaves to escape him but trips. Rhett picks her up, carries her upstairs, and begins to make love to her. Scarlett responds.

She knows now he does love her and thinks she can use this to her advantage. Rhett disappears for two days. He tells Scarlett he's been at Belle's and admits he previously set Belle up in business. He has come to say that he is leaving for Charleston and New Orleans and then points unspecified and to offer her a divorce, providing he can take Bonnie.

When Scarlett tells him Bonnie cannot go with him, he turns on her, informing her he refuses to let her do to Bonnie what she did to Wade and Ella: break her spirit. Scarlett wants to confess to Melly but Melly won't listen, saying no explanation is necessary. She wants desperately to keep Melanie's high opinion of her. For the first time in her life, Scarlett knows she cannot selfishly unburden herself of her guilt because it would mean such unhappiness for Melanie, who thinks the accusation nothing more than a lie concocted by those who are jealous of Scarlett. As she listens, it occurs to Scarlett that Ashley sacrificed his relationship with his sister in order to keep Scarlett's name from being further besmirched. Melanie intends to cut India and Mrs. Elsing cold, knowing full well that this will start a feud.

It is Melly who insists Scarlett go about her usual routine and takes her calling. Those who love Melanie accept it as proof of Scarlett's innocence. Those who believe India feel further vindi-

cated by Rhett's absence. The entire town becomes polarized by the feud. Pittypat is caught in the middle between Scarlett— upon whom she depends financially—and India, who lives with her as a female companion, affording Pittypat the independence of her own home.

During the three months Rhett is gone, Scarlett continues her business, but halfheartedly. She is pregnant and heartsick, avoids Ashley, nags Johnnie Gallegher, and misses Rhett and Bonnie. When they return, Rhett and Scarlett immediately take up where they'd left off—hurting each other. He accuses her of letting Ashley father this baby when she angrily tells him she is pregnant. She makes another angry retort and he suggests she may miscarry, which would solve the problem of having another of his babies. She lunges for him and loses her balance as he sidesteps her attack. This results in her falling then rolling down a flight of stairs. She breaks her rib, bruises her face, hits her head, and miscarries.

During her convalescence she asks only for Melanie, not willing to admit she wants Rhett because she thinks he doesn't want her. Melly splits her time between the delirious Scarlett and a drunken, sobbing, scared Rhett who thinks he killed Scarlett by forcing her to have sex, which resulted in a pregnancy she didn't want. He stops his tormented ravings before he tells Melly that Scarlett never loved him but always Ashley.

Analysis

Scarlett is beginning to understand what she's done to herself and everyone around her. She sees Ashley avoiding her and knows she's not only lost a valued friend but shamed him as well. She knows there will be a feud because Melly refuses to believe India and the feud will be Scarlett's fault. It will divide her family and the town. She thinks about her children and sees clearly how Wade fears her and Ella is something of a fool. She doesn't go so far as to admit to herself that Rhett was right each time he warned her about her selfishness, but she misses him terribly and realizes she loves him.

When she becomes aware of her pregnancy, she allows her pride—not her egocentricity—to prevent her from finding Rhett and telling him. Despite her desire not to have more children, she wants this one because it is Rhett's. She has the time and the money to devote to a child now and she wants to be more like Melly or Rhett with this child instead of the selfish, forbidding parent she's been to Wade and Ella. She misses Bonnie, the child who isn't afraid of her and is most like Rhett.

She also takes her first emotionally mature action: she doesn't confess to Melly. It is suddenly more important to her to spare Melly the pain this confession would bring than to purge her own conscience to make life easier for herself as she usually does. In her delirium after the miscarriage, she confuses herself with Melly in childbirth but each time she thinks it's Melly, she reminds herself she must help Melly and be her strength. Scarlett has one foot firmly in emotional maturity now.

Study Questions

1. Why does Scarlett look for a drink after Ashley's surprise party?

2. What does Rhett tell Scarlett?

3. After disappearing for two days, why does Rhett come home?

4. Why doesn't Scarlett confess to Melly?

5. Why is there a feud?

6. How does Scarlett feel when she discovers she is pregnant?

7. When Rhett returns after three months, what do he and Scarlett immediately begin to do?

8. Why does Scarlett miscarry?

9. What does Rhett do during her illness?

10. In her delirium, about what does Scarlett think?

Answers

1. Ashley's surprise birthday party is a terrible experience for Scarlett. She stands between Melly and Ashley while Ashley looks ashamed and Melly radiates love and trust in her as they greet the guests. Melly frankly shields Scarlett and Ashley from any word of scandal. The thought that she owes

whatever remains of her reputation to Melanie causes Scarlett to crave liquor.

2. A very drunk Rhett gives his wife a drink and tells her he knows all about her secret imbibing and her lust for Ashley.

3. Rhett intimates he's been at Belle's for the past two days and has come home only to pack and get Bonnie and Prissy. He's taking them on an extended trip beginning with Charleston and New Orleans. He also tells her he'll never approach her sexually again and she may have a divorce if she chooses, providing he gets Bonnie. He attacks her motherhood as being nothing more than bullying.

4. At first Scarlett doesn't confess to Melly because Melly wants no explanations and won't listen. But, while Scarlett needs to confess to ease her mind, she knows she cannot risk Melly's high opinion of her and must not be selfish enough to destroy Melly's life with this confession.

5. Melly refuses to believe India. She thinks India hates Scarlett because she is jealous of her looks and former beaux, especially Stuart Tarleton. Melly refuses to allow India into her home anymore or be in any home where she is being received.

6. Scarlett is glad to be pregnant with Rhett's child, who was conceived the night of Ashley's surprise party. A drunken Rhett attempted to take her first by force, although she enjoyed it after the first few moments. She wants a boy to spend her time and money on.

7. No sooner is Rhett in the house after a three month absence than he and Scarlett are at each other's throats.

8. When Rhett mentions a miscarriage, Scarlett becomes dizzy at the memory of the pain of childbirth and angry that he has no idea how much it hurts. She lunges for him. As he sidesteps to protect himself, she loses her balance and pitches backward, then rolls down the flight of stairs upon which they are standing.

9. Rhett is drunk and tormented during most of Scarlett's ill-

ness, thinking she is going to die and that he caused her death.

10. In her delirium, Scarlett thinks about childbirth, hers and Melly's. When she thinks it is Melly giving birth, she also thinks of Atlanta burning, the Yankees coming, and how she must stay in Atlanta with Melly to be strong for her during the birth. Either way, she keeps feeling the stabs of pain.

Chapters 57-59

Summary

A month later, Rhett sends Scarlett home to Tara at her request. Wade and Ella go too, minded by Prissy. Melanie avoids Rhett, embarrassed by what he's told her in his drunkenness the night Scarlett began to recover. He comes to see her, to find out what the problem is, and to ask a favor: he wants Melly to help him persuade Ashley to take the money from him to buy the other half of the mill he shares with Scarlett and purchase her other mill.

Rhett fears for Scarlett's health when she returns home and works as hard as she had before her illness. Rhett feels the store will be strenuous enough work for her but knows she won't sell the mills to anyone but Ashley. He wants Melly to deceive both Ashley and Scarlett by not telling them where the money comes from when he sends it to Ashley.

Scarlett, who is now in good health, and the children return, to be met by Rhett. Scarlett chatters on with news of the country. When she asks what is new in Atlanta, Rhett tells her Ashley wants to buy the mills. Apparently, someone he nursed though smallpox at the military prison camp on Rock Island sent him money; Ashley doesn't know who. Then Rhett manipulates her into agreeing to the sale. She suspects he may have a hand in this but he denies it.

Ashley buys the mills, refusing to take advantage of Scarlett's low asking price, and there is a small ceremony. She immediately regrets selling them and is dismayed to hear Ashley say he will return the convicts and use "free darkie" labor instead. Ashley and Rhett agree with each other that this is best. She becomes angry with Ashley, but quiets herself as it dawns on her that she doesn't understand Ashley nor is she like him. During her argument with Ashley, Rhett points out that the money she has made has not made her happy. She finds she cannot disagree.

After her recovery, Rhett is distantly polite to Scarlett but doesn't seem to care for her anymore. His attention is redirected from Scarlett to Bonnie. Scarlett is jealous of her favorite child. Rhett no longer drinks and is home for supper more often. Scarlett notices his friends now are those who were Frank's during the days of Klan activity and fears he is involved in the Klan. When she asks him, he tells her Ashley and he were mainly responsible for the Klan's disbanding. She is relieved to hear he won't die the way Frank did, but then he proceeds to tell her he's helping to imprison some of their old Republican friends and using the Confederate gold he's been holding since the war to help elect a Democrat. He insists he will keep taking Bonnie with him to Democratic political meetings.

Bullock flees North, arranging for his resignation to be announced once he is safe. It is almost certain a Democratic governor will be elected. While the Scalawags, Carpetbaggers, and Republicans are fearful, the Old Guard is quietly jubilant.

It is obvious Bonnie is wild and that Rhett is no help in taming her. She has complete domination over her father, which undermines any attempts Scarlett makes at disciplining her. The children acquire a pony when Bonnie is four years old. It is to be shared by all of them, but Wade prefers his dog and Ella is afraid of animals. Once Rhett is assured Bonnie knows how to ride well, he teaches her and the pony how to take low jumps. Bonnie loves it but requests a higher bar. She is told she may have this when she is six. For once, Rhett insists, only to give way in the face of one of her tantrums. As Rhett and Scarlett watch Bonnie try to jump this higher bar, Scarlett has a premonition and tries to stop Bonnie from jumping, but it is too late. Bonnie breaks her neck in the fall. Scarlett blames Rhett for her death.

The children stay at Melanie's while they all await the arrival of Rhett's mother so they may bury Bonnie. Mammy comes to Melanie and breaks down crying. Rhett won't let them bury Bonnie. He is drunk and orders all the shutters thrown open and the lamps lit for he has placed Bonnie on her bed beside his and thinks she's still afraid of the dark. He's spent the last two days at Belle's and

the nights in his room with Bonnie. He threatens to kill Scarlett if she attempts to bury Bonnie the next day as she says she will. Mammy begs Melly to intercede with Rhett.

Analysis

While Scarlett struggles with Bonnie's death, selling her mills, and realizing money has not made her happy, Rhett falls apart at his beloved daughter's death. He has been able to overcome rumors, being ousted by his father, living outside the law, ostracism, a marriage to Scarlett, but not the loss of his daughter. When Scarlett accuses him of murdering Bonnie, he doesn't deny it but simply thinks her heartless.

Having transferred his love from his wife to his daughter and reshaping his life solely for her benefit, he cannot accept the death of his purpose for living. While there is no doubt he loves Bonnie, he is also obsessed by her. It is for her he stops drinking, begins working in his bank, cultivates the Old Guard matriarchs, and turns Democrat. For all his strength in dealing with Scarlett, the war, and the townspeople, he is not strong enough to lose Bonnie.

This is the first time Rhett is not a realist. He denies her death by insisting the lamps be lit, the shutters be thrown open, Bonnie be placed on her bed in his room, and refusing to allow her to be buried. In his temporary madness, he cannot understand why they insist upon a funeral and threatens to kill Scarlett should she try to bury Bonnie. His world has collapsed and he with it. Only Mammy realizes he is out of his mind with grief.

Study Questions

1. Why does Rhett come to see Melanie?
2. What is the "cover story" for the money?
3. About what do Rhett and Ashley agree?
4. About what can Scarlett not disagree?
5. Why does she fear Rhett is involved in the Klan?
6. What does Rhett buy for the children?
7. What does Bonnie love to do?

8. Why do the children stay at Melanie's home?

9. Why does Mammy come to speak with Melly?

10. Why won't Rhett allow Bonnie to be buried?

Answers

1. Rhett thinks the store will be enough to keep Scarlett occupied without tiring her out. He is worried about her health. He also knows the only person she will sell the mills to is Ashley. He wants Melanie to deceive Ashley and Scarlett by not telling them Rhett gave Ashley the money to use in purchasing the mills from Scarlett. Melanie agrees only when Rhett impresses upon her that she needs the money to provide for her son.

2. When Melanie explains to Rhett she cannot say the money is from one of her relatives because they don't have any money, he arranges to send the money to Ashley along with a letter saying it's from someone he nursed through smallpox while imprisoned at Rock Island.

3. Rhett and Ashley agree that "free darkie" labor is more palatable than convict labor.

4. Rhett sarcastically asks if the money Scarlett earns using convict labor, or from her saloon property, makes her happy. While she knows it has enabled her to be warm, dress well, eat enough, and educate her son, she cannot disagree when it is implied that she is still not happy despite having this money.

5. Rhett stays out late more and more often and brings friends home with him when he returns.

6. When Bonnie is four, Rhett buys a pony for the children.

7. Bonnie loves to jump. Once assured she can ride well, Rhett has hurdles built in the backyard.

8. The family is waiting for Rhett's mother to arrive so Bonnie may be buried.

9. Mammy is beside herself. Rhett has spent two days at Belle's

only coming home at night to keep Bonnie's body company in his well lit room. He is constantly drunk and will not allow his daughter to be buried.

10. Bonnie was afraid of the dark. In Rhett's crazed mind, he knows he cannot let her be buried, because it is too dark in a grave.

Chapters 60-63

Summary

Scarlett is fearful. She sees she can expect no solace from Rhett. While she wants to apologize for saying he murdered Bonnie, the longer she waits, the harder it is to do. He is becoming a silent, morose, untidy drunk who is rarely at home. Dr. Meade advises Scarlett to have another baby with Rhett so he will stop this drinking which will eventually kill him and which he does to forget the pain of his daughter's death. Mammy goes back to Tara permanently, so the lonely Scarlett has only Melanie with whom to talk.

From the Old Guard, only Pittypat, Melanie, and Ashley call on Scarlett. She discounts the visits from her new friends saying they don't know her. Scarlett finally understands why ex-Confederates talk of the war so much; it is to remind themselves they've been through terrible days and survived. She realizes that she has let these kinds of friends slip away from her and misses them now.

While she is in Marietta, Rhett sends Scarlett a telegram which causes her to leave Wade and Ella in the hotel with Prissy and return to Atlanta immediately. Melanie is dying of a miscarriage. Rhett is the only one who knew she is pregnant, solely because only he surmised why she suddenly became so happy. After meeting her at the train, Rhett takes Scarlett to Melanie's house and leaves without entering himself. India, Pittypat, and Ashley are there. Ashley tells her Melly's been asking for her and Scarlett sees in his face that Melanie is indeed dying but refuses to accept it. He explains Melly wanted to keep the pregnancy a secret until she was certain it was safe.

Dr. Meade enters from Melanie's room. He spies Scarlett and contemptuously tells her Melly wants to see her. They all want to see Melanie but Dr. Meade escorts Scarlett into her room, warning her not to make any confessions about Ashley. Once Scarlett sees her, she accepts that Melly is dying.

As Scarlett thinks to herself that she must not let Melly go, Melly gives her Beau—for the second time, reminding Scarlett that before he was born, Melly made her promise to take him if she should die during childbirth. Scarlett begs Melly to try not to die, all the while superstitiously thinking she's killed her by wishing so often she would die. Melly asks Scarlett to look after Ashley and his business without letting him know but, at first, Scarlett misunderstands and thinks Melly has known her feelings for Ashley all along. Dr. Meade calls her out of the room but not before Melly tells Scarlett to be kind to Rhett, he loves her. A saddened Scarlett acknowledges to herself that she's losing the only woman friend she ever had.

Scarlett looks for Ashley, finding him in his room. She asks him to hold her because she's so frightened but he tells her he was just wanting her to hold him for the same reason. Scarlett lashes out at him for not realizing Melly is worth a million "Scarletts" and for only wanting Scarlett in a physical way. She sees in his face that he knows she is right and regrets berating him right after she'd promised she'd take care of him. She comforts him as he cries, feeling his strength—meaning Melly—is gone and promises to help him manage.

Dr. Meade calls for Ashley. Scarlett is surprised to discover she doesn't feel hurt upon learning Ashley never loved her. She no longer wants him but must honor her deathbed promise to Melanie to watch over him.

All of the others look to Scarlett for orders. She knows she must pull herself together and make arrangements for Melanie's funeral. Saying she needs to be alone for a moment, she flees home. As she walks, she recognizes the mist as the one from her nightmare. As in her dream, she begins to run. She sees home and realizes that's where she wants to be and Rhett is the security she's been looking for, not Ashley. She sees how stupid and blind she's been all these years. She continues running, this time not away from her nightmare, but toward who she sees as her refuge—Rhett.

When she first arrives home, she cannot find him. Then she locates him, sober, in the dining room. He asks if Melly is dead, stopping Scarlett from the declaration of love for him she was going to make. He tells her he didn't go in the house with her because he could not bear to see Melly dying. He is surprised to hear Scarlett tell him how much she loves Melly. Scarlett tells him Melly's last words to her. She also tells him Melly requested she take care of Beau and Ashley.

Rhett misconstrues what she is saying and expects Scarlett to divorce him in order to marry Ashley. She protests but he knows since she decided she's wrong about Ashley, she also decided she loves him. Rhett explains his love for her has worn out so it's simply no use to go on, although it is obvious they were meant for each other. When she offers to make it up to him, to have babies with him, he refuses, not willing to risk his heart a third time. He feels only pity and kindness for her.

Rhett is leaving but promises to come back often enough to stave off gossip since Scarlett wants neither a divorce nor a separation. When she asks what she should do without him, he responds he doesn't care. Rather than face her loss of both Rhett and Ashley in addition to Melanie's death, Scarlett plans to go home to Tara the next day.

Analysis

As the book ends, Scarlett sees she has thrown away everyone who is really important to her through her narcissism, her selfishness, her egocentricity. Melanie, her only female friend, dies with Scarlett appreciating her only on her death bed. The Old Guard, who know her and share her history, want nothing to do with her. She finally understands that she made up the Ashley she had loved; the actual Ashley is nothing like the one she'd dreamed of. And Rhett, the person she now sees as her refuge, no longer loves her. She has effectively worn out his love with her lusting after Ashley, her temper tantrums, her disregard of her children, and her focus on herself. Even Mammy has left for Tara permanently.

Throughout her life, Scarlett thinks she will be happy if only . . . she has enough to eat . . . or more than enough money . . . or Ashley . . . or, finally, Rhett. Each time, once she reaches her goal, she is not happy. The quest for whatever it is keeps her strong but there is no pot of gold at the end of the rainbow for her. She returns to her magical, "I'll think of it tomorrow," but there is part of her that knows tomorrow never comes for her. She is a lonely, unfulfilled woman with no visible hope in front of her. As Rhett says he is leaving, she asks what she will do without him but he has no answer for her and no longer cares. While Scarlett succeeds in facing reality, both in the literal sense and emotionally, it is a painful journey for her and it is not over.

Study Questions

1. How does Rhett react to Bonnie's death?
2. Why does Rhett call Scarlett back to Atlanta from Marietta?
3. Why won't Rhett go into Melanie's house?
4. What is it Dr. Meade warns Scarlett not to do?
5. What does Melanie ask Scarlett to do?
6. What does Ashley want from Scarlett?
7. What is it Scarlett realizes about her feelings for Ashley?
8. What do Pittypat, India, Ashley, and the others expect Scarlett to do?
9. As she runs home, what happens to Scarlett?
10. Why is Rhett leaving?

Answers

1. After Bonnie's funeral, Rhett becomes a distant drunk who is never home. He is untidy and forgets to change his clothes.
2. Rhett sends Scarlett a telegram stating Melanie is ill and to return immediately from Marietta.
3. He cannot bear to see her dying so he does not go into the house after bringing Scarlett there from the train station.
4. A contemptuous and disapproving Dr. Meade sees Scarlett and ushers her in to see Melanie, warning her this is not the time for a confession about Ashley.
5. Melanie asks Scarlett to look after Beau, to see he goes to college, to secretly look after Ashley's health and business, and to be kind to Rhett.

6. Scarlett looks for Ashley, wanting him to comfort her but he needs comfort from her.

7. Scarlett realizes Ashley is frightened and not strong. She abruptly realizes he has only wanted her body, as Rhett said. She knows Ashley doesn't love her and really doesn't care.

8. Pittypat, India, Ashley, and the others expect Scarlett to tell them what to do to prepare for Melanie's funeral.

9. Without planning to, Scarlett finds herself running through the mist toward her own home. She recognizes this mist as the one in her nightmare. There was no light or refuge in her dream but she sees a light in this mist and thinks of the refuge of home—and Rhett.

10. Rhett says his love for Scarlett is worn out.

Suggested Essay Topics

1. Rhett is one of the most complex characters in the novel. After describing his "public persona" as seen by the townspeople and both armies, how would you contrast this with the "private persona" seen only by his wife, family, and servants?

2. What does Scarlett's choice of Scalawags and Carpetbaggers as her friends and her choices for the new house tell you about the Reconstructionist government influencing some Southerners into building a false society during the Reconstructionist period?

3. Including The Ladies' Sewing Circle for the Widows and Orphans of the Confederacy and Scarlett's "crush" in your explanation, describe how the war caused rifts between friends, families, and neighbors.

4. Surprisingly, Melanie does "bad" to do "good." Extrapolating from her past relationship with Scarlett, explain how Rhett convinces her to lie to both Ashley and Scarlett about the source of funds for Ashley to buy Scarlett's half of the mill he owns with her, as well as the second mill.

Sample Analytical Paper Topics

The following paper topics are based on the entire novel. Following each topic is an outline to help get you started.

Topic #1

Until recently, historians have glorified war—especially the returning soldiers. How has Margaret Mitchell repudiated this idea with her novel?

Outline

I. Thesis Statement: *In* Gone With The Wind, *Margaret Mitchell rejects the glorification of war through her vivid depiction of the negative aspects of the Civil War.*

II. Shortage of Goods

   A. Soaring Prices

   B. Unable to get past Yankee blockades to get cash crops to England for sale

III. Loss of Existing Lifestyle

   A. Scarlett's "mourning period" for her first husband cut short

   B. Plantations burned to the ground (the Mallory house, Twelve Oaks)

    C. Scarlett comes to the realization that everything her mother and Mammy had taught her about being a "lady" is of no use in the war-ravaged South

IV. Death Toll

    A. Friends and loved one's names appear on casualty lists

        1. Brent, Stuart and Thomas Tarleton, Joe Fontaine, Dallas McLure, Darcy Meade, etc.

    B. Jonesboro is lost and Scarlett sees wounded and dying men all around her

V. Occupation by Union Army

    A. Atlanta is burned

    B. Yankee soldiers take everything of value—jewelry, money, weapons, and ruin everything they can't steal

Topic #2

The Civil War radically changed the city of Atlanta. It went from being the center of Southern aristocracy, through the ravages of war, to a post-war boom town. Compare the changes to the city for each of the three stages with the changes that occurred at the O'Hara plantation, Tara.

Outline

I. Thesis Statement: *The fortunes of Atlanta reflect those of Tara and in effect, those of Scarlett.*

II. Pre-War

    A. Atlanta as seat of Southern aristocracy

    B. "Old South" values

    C. Master and slave relationship

III. War

    A. Burning of Atlanta/Ravages of Tara

    B. Increasing role-leadership of women

IV. Post-war

A. Rebuilding of Atlanta

B. Influx of new industry

C. Occupation by Union army—Yankee searches

D. Role of the freed slave

Topic #3

Compare the relationship between Scarlett and Rhett with that between Ashley and Melanie.

Outline

I. Thesis Statement: *Although the relationship between Scarlett and Rhett may seem a direct contrast to the relationship between Melanie and Ashley, there are many parallels as well. In addition, there is a parallel admiration between Rhett and Melanie and Scarlett and Ashley.*

II. Differences

A. Scarlett and Rhett have fiery, volatile relationship, founded on mutual feelings of love and hat.

1. Frequent arguments and verbal sparring

2. Matching of wits

B. Melanie and Ashley have a quiet, gentle, and mundane relationship, founded on friendship, closeness, and trust

III. Similarities

A. In the end, Scarlett's love for Rhett is as true as Melanie's love for Ashley

B. Scarlett's feelings for Ashley and Ashley's for Scarlett

1. Scarlett's juvenile obsessive worship of Ashley, based on his "goodness"—his looks, kindness and being a "gentleman"

2. Ashley's initial denial of any feelings towards Scarlett

3. Ashley's admission of feelings for Scarlett, and the events leading up to it

    C.   Rhett's feelings for Melanie and and Melanie's for Rhett

        1.   Rhett's admiration of Melanie's quiet strength

        2.   Melanie's unconditional forgiveness

Topic #4

Margaret Mitchell spends a great deal of time describing "The Old South," including its traditions and conventions, in Part I of the novel. The destruction and breakdown of these practices, as a result of the War, is alluded to and detailed in the remainder of the novel. Discuss how the War led to a reversal of roles in the Old South.

Outline

I.   Thesis Statement: *As a result of the Civil War, the relationships between rich and poor, male and female, and slave and master were reversed.*

II.   Rich and Poor

    A.   Life of the plantation families is contrasted with that of "poor whites," as with Emmie Slattery's illegitimate child

    B.   After loss of their plantations and money after the war, aristocracy finds themselves in similar financial circumstances as the "poor whites"

III.   The ending of slavery changes the roles played by the aristocracy and their former slaves

    A.   Mammy no longer has to obey Scarlett's commands

    B.   Rhett is jailed for killing a freed slave who insulted a white woman

IV.   Male and female roles

    A.   Scarlett is now head of the family

        1.   runs Tara

        2.   operates sawmill

    B.   Ashley is reduced to working for Scarlett

SECTION EIGHT

Bibliography

Athearn, Robert G. *American Heritage New Illustrated History of the United States, Volumes 7 & 8.* New York: American Heritage Publishing Co., 1963.

Lingley, Charles Ramsdell, and Foley, Allen Richard. *Since the Civil War—Third Edition.* New York: Century Co., Inc., 1935.

Mitchell, Margaret. Gone *with the Wind.* New York: Warner Books, 1964.

Morison, Samuel Eliot, Commager, Henry Steele, and Lenchtenburg, William E. *A Concise History of the American Republic.* New York: Oxford University Press, 1983.

Stampp, Kenneth M. *The Era of Reconstruction 1865-1877.* New York: Alfred A. Knopf, 1966.

Introducing...

MAXnotes

REA's Literature Study Guides

MAXnotes™ offer a fresh look at masterpieces of literature, presented in a lively and interesting fashion. **MAXnotes**™ offer the essentials of what you should know about the work, including outlines, explanations and discussions of the plot, character lists, analyses, and historical context. **MAXnotes**™ are designed to help you think independently about literary works by raising various issues and thought-provoking ideas and questions. Written by literary experts who currently teach the subject, **MAXnotes**™ enhance your understanding and enjoyment of the work.

Available **MAXnotes**™ include the following:

Gone With The Wind
by Margaret Mitchell

The Grapes of Wrath
by John Steinbeck

Great Expectations
by Charles Dickens

The Great Gatsby
by F. Scott Fitzgerald

Hamlet
by William Shakespeare

Huckleberry Finn
by Mark Twain

**I Know Why the
Caged Bird Sings**
by Maya Angelou

Julius Caesar
by William Shakespeare

Les Misèrables
by Victor Hugo

Macbeth
by William Shakespeare

The Odyssey
by Homer

A Raisin in the Sun
by Lorraine Hansberry

The Scarlet Letter
by Nathaniel Hawthorne

A Tale of Two Cities
by Charles Dickens

To Kill a Mockingbird
by Harper Lee

RESEARCH & EDUCATION ASSOCIATION
61 Ethel Road W. • Piscataway, New Jersey 08854
Phone: (908) 819-8880

Please send me more information about MAXnotes™.

Name _____

Address _____

City _____ State _____ Zip _____

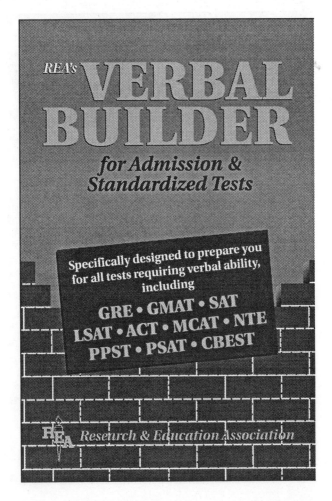